THE OTHER MOTHER

THE OTHER MOTHER

A Woman's Love for the Child
She Gave Up for Adoption

CAROL SCHAEFER

Published by
Soho Press, Inc.
1 Union Square
New York N.Y. 10003

Library of Congress Cataloging-in-Publication Data

Schaefer, Carol, 1946–
The other mother: a woman's love for the child
she gave up for adoption/by Carol Schaefer.

p.   cm.
ISBN 0–939149–41–9
1. Schaefer, Carol, 1946–   . 2. Unmarried mothers—United
States—Biography. 3. Adoption—United States—Case studies. 4.
Children, Adopted—United States—Biography. I. Title.

HV700.5.S33   1991
362.83'92'092—dc20
[B]   90–39201
CIP

Design and Composition by The Sarabande Press

Manufactured in the United States of America

For my sons Jack, Brett and Kip.

"*Can a mother forget her infant? Be without love for the fruit of her womb? Even should she forget, I would not forget.*"

Isaiah 49:15

THE OTHER MOTHER

Chapter One

The year was 1965.

We sat in the dark hardwood chairs centered in front of the sister's desk. The venetian blinds covering the large window behind the desk were three-quarters shut. The light made a pattern of narrow streaks on the ceiling. None fell across Sister Dominic's black habit. On my right, Mom leaned forward, eager for the sister to know we were there to do the right thing. Then this mortal sin would be erased from my soul and hers, too. My penance would be to go to the home for unwed mothers. Absolution would come after I gave up my baby. Sister was telling us that I would forget everything. It would be as if it had never happened.

The chair slats dug into my back as I leaned against them for support. Sister Dominic sat turned toward my mother, her right shoulder pointing accusingly toward me. Neither one of them saw me as separate from my mother. I felt paralyzed, unable to speak up for myself. I wanted my mother to leave the room. There were things I wanted to say to the sister, questions

I wanted to ask: Was there any way to keep my baby? Was there anyone who would help me find a way to do that?

We had been given a form to fill out while we waited outside her office for Sister Dominic to see us, to keep the appointment my mother had made with Catholic Social Services to work out arrangements for my admission to Seton House. Mom had answered most of the questions on the form for me. I couldn't resist; I had done enough by getting pregnant and ruining everyone's life. I felt that I risked losing everyone's love. I was not as afraid of the Church's recriminations as my mother was. But, fearing abandonment, I acquiesced in the abandonment of my own baby.

"Do you want the child raised Catholic?"

"Oh yes, of course, Sister," my mother obediently responded, as if answering a catechism question.

"Do you prefer that the parents be college graduates?"

"Absolutely," I answered, finally finding enough strength to speak.

"Of course, we will perfectly match your child according to ethnic background," Sister assured us. I felt a little uncomfortable since we weren't completely certain what all our roots were. "They will have a good income and provide everything your baby needs. You can be quite certain of that," she told us. And, of course, since my baby's father, Chris, and I both had blue eyes, the parents would have blue eyes, she said. Sister smiled benevolently, cocking her head up slightly as if already putting her order in to God.

The parents would reflect Chris and me in every way; the baby would miss out on nothing by not being with us. In fact, Catholic Social Services would find parents who would be able to provide far more for our baby than Chris and I ever could. Chris and I would be able to finish school and, if we decided to

4

marry then, go on to have other children. Clearly, I was doing the best—the only—thing, by giving the baby up for adoption.

I kept wishing my mother would leave the room so I could speak with Sister alone. I wanted to know what would happen if I were to change my mind. But my mother did not leave my side.

We signed the papers and then it was settled. My exact arrival date would be determined by the availability of space at Seton House. The home accommodated a maximum of sixteen girls, and my admission would depend on births occurring on schedule. But I could count on being received there sometime in October.

Sister Dominic leaned forward, and hands pressed against her desk top, pushed herself erect. Her black habit added stature to her above-average height. She seemed to tower over us.

As my Mom and I stood, the edges in the room seemed to blur. I heard their voices as if from a distance. Could this really be happening to me?

———

How had I gotten into this fix? The way any girl, even a nice Catholic girl, did.

When I was a junior in high school, my best friend was Jessica. We did what everyone in our North Carolina town did that summer: drove over to the Boar and Castle Drive-in parking area to meet our friends and, sometimes, make new ones. The parking area was divided into two sections. The left side was brightly lit for cruising and socializing. The right side was dim and silent. It was called the "Snake Pit." All the windows of the cars parked on this side were steamed up, creating the effect of drawn curtains. This evening, Jessica and I checked out the Snake Pit and then parked her father's huge powder blue Buick under a big maple tree on the left side of the lot so her boyfriend, Michael, couldn't miss us. Michael worked the night shift at a bookbinding plant. He was to meet us during his break.

When he drove up, he had someone I didn't recognize in the passenger seat of his Austin-Healy. When Michael hopped into the backseat of the Buick behind Jessica, his friend slid into the seat behind me. As I turned to meet Michael's friend, the first thing I noticed about him was his hands. They gripped the plush-covered front seat as he pulled himself forward to be introduced. He had beautiful hands. Then, as the light revealed his face to me, I saw he had a great smile, a smile that reached his eyes. I had an almost irresistible urge to touch his hands. I knew they would feel familiar. But I resisted.

His name was Chris. He was a sophomore in college. Well, that ended it. I was forbidden to date anyone in college. My Dad would *never* allow us to go out. But I felt as if time were suspended inside Jessica's powder blue Buick. I wanted, I *really* wanted, to get to know Chris. Back at our friend Cindy's house, I threw myself across her bed in a teenage surrender to love.

After the night we met at the Castle, Chris and I each discreetly dispatched our personal emissaries, Jessica and Michael, to see if the other was interested in dating. The feelings were definitely mutual. The familiarity I had sensed at first sight was still there on our first date and never went away. When they met him, my parents liked him even though he was older and not a Catholic. We dated all the way through my senior year. Chris would come home from college almost every other weekend. Our feelings for each other just kept growing.

There was a strict peer code in the South in the sixties that kept our passion for each other in check. Everything was seen as either black or white. You were a good girl or a bad girl, which meant you either went all the way or you didn't, no matter how long you were involved with someone. You lived in the right neighborhood or the wrong one, belonged to the right country club or the wrong one, or worse, none. You wore Villager blouses and Weejuns or you were out. We first moved to North Carolina when I was in ninth grade. I had been attending a Catholic girls' school in Ohio and I went to my new school wearing canvas Keds because that was what was "in" up there in Ohio. When Jessica and I first became close friends, she confided in me that some kids had thought I was poor because I wore Keds. And being poor was not good.

The double standard was deeply ingrained. If a boy got close to the imaginary border of going too far with a "good" girl, the instincts of a Southern gentleman would stir and the vagrant hand or passionate thought would be brought under control. The reservoir of self-discipline we must have cultivated by passionately making out to Johnny Mathis for four straight hours without trying "first base" probably contributed greatly to our collective character development.

The night I became pregnant was the second time Chris and I had made love and probably the hundredth time we had fought it in the two years we'd been going together. By then I was a freshman at Winthrop College, a women's college in South Carolina. We were both home for Easter vacation. Because of midterms we hadn't seen each other for over a month, the longest time we had been apart since we'd begun dating. That night we had only a little time to be with each other. It was Good Friday and I had to go to the stations of the cross first.

We parked Chris's aqua Ford Galaxy in the lower parking lot

of the Greenwood country club, near the tennis courts. Because it was Good Friday, the lot was deserted. The sky was pitch black, it seemed, perfectly suited for a Good Friday night. The stations of the cross always affected me deeply. We talked. Our feelings for each other just got too intense to be controlled.

I was too caught up to utter a warning. Afterwards, Chris got out of the car, then stuck his head back through the window and asked me if it was a bad time of the month for me. He said the condom had broken. But I was always irregular and hadn't had a period in four months. I told him not to worry.

When a month went by and still no period arrived, *I* began to worry. I was not feeling my usual self. I didn't want to go to a local doctor so I made an appointment with my roommate Blair's older sister's gynecologist in Charlotte. But at Winthrop a freshman wasn't allowed to travel farther than twenty-five miles from campus without parental permission. I got caught coming back and the school called my parents. In a couple of hours, my mother was on the phone to me, telling me she had found and spoken with the gynecologist. So much for "patient confidentiality." The test, however, was negative. I was restricted to campus until the end of the year. I resented being treated by the school, my parents, and the doctor as if I were a child, but to them, that's what I was.

Chris was relieved that the test was negative. But I didn't feel so certain.

I was under so much stress that my exams went badly. My parents' faces were grim when I got home. But nothing was said, except that my mother asked if I had gotten my period yet. I said no.

This was the situation my dad had dreaded, sitting up countless nights in the big aqua chair in the living room waiting for me to come home. Most times as I came in the door from a date I'd found him asleep in the chair, light from the brass floor lamp falling on the book or newspaper he had been reading to keep himself awake. I'd be grounded for six weeks straight if I was five minutes past curfew, probably because he needed a rest from worry and nights spent in that big aqua chair. I felt a tenderness for him but also a great anger that he felt I couldn't be trusted. He would say that he trusted *me*, but he didn't trust the guys I was dating.

Now my father forbade me to see Chris again. I had to see Chris, so we would meet secretly.

Another month went by. I was feeling fine except still no period. It was the end of June. Chris had a connection at the hospital; we could get the test repeated quietly.

This time it was positive.

We didn't talk until we reached the hospital parking lot. The sun was beating down hard on the black asphalt. The humidity made it feel like we were walking through thickened air. I wanted to distance myself from the facts, but the hot air conspired to keep us locked into the real world. It was too hot to get into the car to talk. We stood there. It was hard to grasp the reality of what still seemed so unreal. Except for missed periods, and the test, I wouldn't have known I was pregnant. I had no symptoms. My body hadn't changed. Chris was looking at the same person he'd always known. Yet nothing was the same, or ever would be again.

The only way to get an abortion was to fly down to the Bahamas. I could just see myself doing that! We could never get the money anyway without telling our parents, and I knew my mother would *never* allow me to have an abortion. Chris had not mentioned marriage yet. Would I marry him if he did? Standing on the hot black asphalt, my feet nearly seared, I found myself playing over in my head a "tape" of all the comments I had heard about the situation I was in. Boys laughed at girls who got "knocked up" as tramps. People talked about women "trapping" men into marrying them by getting pregnant. Would Chris always wonder? Would I always wonder if he loved me? Where did these questions originate? Certainly not in my heart. But I didn't trust my heart.

We decided to tell our parents.

I asked my mother to come into my room the next morning. I was sitting on the floor next to a patch of sunshine. I told her simply and straight out that I had had a positive pregnancy test. I knew it wasn't really a surprise to her. With not one clue, she had figured out that I violated the twenty-five-mile restriction at Winthrop because I had gone to a doctor to see if I were pregnant. She seemed able to divine that from the clear blue sky, so how could she be surprised now? She wasn't. But she was still shocked.

"You must have been drunk," she said.

I said, "No, I was completely sober."

"I don't believe that," she said, "you had to have been drunk."

"No, Mom, I wasn't," I said as clearly as I could. I wanted to add, "I was in love," but those words wouldn't come out of my mouth. Why did she have to assume I would have had to be drunk? Would that magically excuse me, even restore my virginity? Was she afraid for the mortal sin on my soul?

"Is Chris going to marry you?" she asked. I told her that I didn't know. She left the room to talk to Dad. The patch of sunshine on the floor had moved. I sat there for a long time watching it move farther and farther away.

A deep anger was knitted into my father's brow and a great sadness filled his eyes. He was so hurt. I wanted to disappear. "Your mother and I will help you and Chris any way we can," he said. "We always felt you two would marry one day. We will even help pay for Chris's last year at college, if that is the only way he can finish."

I was overwhelmed at their generous acceptance of the situation. With three younger children to think of, I knew it wouldn't be easy for them to swing it financially. Dad said he wanted to talk with Chris's parents. And so they arranged to meet the next day after church.

While our parents met, Jessica and I drove around aimlessly in her dad's blue Buick. The sun, though extremely hot, seemed dull. We swung by the Castle to get a Coke, but it was so hot out that the Castle was deserted. I wondered what our parents were saying to each other. I wondered what Chris was doing. I don't think that either set of parents ever considered that Chris and I ought to be in on their meeting. It was *our* future they were discussing, after all. My mind wandered back to times I had read about when marriages were always arranged affairs, business deals between the heads of families, where the children had no say in their own fate.

After a few hours, we passed by our house. Chris's parents' car was gone. Jessica let me out. I walked up the driveway slowly. It was odd to think that Chris's parents had been in my home. I knew Chris had a good relationship with them, but somehow we had never met.

"They seemed like nice people," my father said, as I let myself in the door. "I offered them everything I told you. The decision is in their hands."

Chris called the next night. Could I meet him at the Castle in a half hour? I borrowed the car and flew out the door. As I drove down familiar streets in our white Chevy Impala, everything suddenly seemed dangerous in the darkness. I began to feel afraid. I slowed the car down. All of a sudden, I was not in such a hurry to see Chris.

I pulled up next to his car, parked on the Snake Pit side of the Castle. Before he had a chance to get out of his car, I let myself into it. Although I hadn't turned to face him, my body already knew. When I finally did look up, our eyes met and held. My head began turning back and forth, saying no, no, before he had spoken a word.

He wanted me to know that the decision was entirely his own and that his parents promised to back him no matter what the outcome. His father had given him the advice that he planned to follow, however. He had said to Chris, that with such a bad start, our marriage would never last. To begin a marriage in debt to parents, not able to stand on our own two feet for who knows how long, and with a new baby to take care of, would doom us. He was sure we would get married "in a few years." This was the wrong way and the wrong time.

I turned away from Chris in anger. All around us were picture-perfect homes sitting on impeccably manicured lawns, but the occupants had their problems, some embarrassing, some worse. No one had a trouble-free life. What was wrong with struggle? Was the measure of a successful life the avoidance of problems? I just knew we could make it. Why did *they* say we couldn't? As I released the deep breath I had taken, I dissolved into sobs I thought would never stop.

My father had said if Chris refused to do the right thing by me, he could never see me again. But I didn't know what to do with the love I still felt for Chris. It was impossible for me to tell Chris to drive off out of my life forever. Yet my father's doubts about Chris's love for me began to gnaw at me.

I told Chris that from now on we would have to make our arrangements to see each other through Jessica or Cindy. Chris promised not to abandon me.

I drove home in a state of shock. I held my hand over my

belly praying our baby would never feel rejected, would never feel such anguish. I walked into the house and told my parents, without looking them in the eyes, that we weren't getting married. Then I went to bed. I passed a sleepless night.

A few days later Chris and I and another couple met secretly over a red-and-white-checked table against the back wall of a roadside lounge called The Jokers Three. Each time the door opened from the main dancing room, wisps of the Beatles, the Temptations, or Johnny Mathis floated into the back room. The Jokers Three had been our favorite place. It was always packed. We had danced for hours on the sawdust-covered floors. But this was the first time I had been in the back room. The light was dim and the walls seemed full of secrets. The gold of the pitcher of Budweiser seemed to glow like a crystal ball in the center of the table. Ted, a good friend of Chris's, and Ted's cousin, Sarah, sat across from us. I had not seen Sarah for a long time. I was fascinated by her. She was very beautiful and blonde, but that wasn't it. She had changed a great deal. There was a strength to her, yet a great sadness. Only a couple of months earlier she had given birth to a daughter and had given her up for adoption. Since I had discovered I was pregnant, I prayed I would have a son, so I would know he would be strong enough to handle being adopted. I was afraid a daughter never could.

Sarah told us about the small home for unwed mothers she had gone to in Richmond, Virginia. I was relieved to know there was an alternative to a Florence Crittendon "factory," a chain of homes for unwed mothers, which I heard each held seventy girls at a time.

As she spoke, I brushed a tear away with my right hand. I didn't want anyone to see me cry. Chris held on tightly to my left hand, as if he or I were going to float away. I stared at the golden

13

glow from the pitcher as if it would reveal some truth to us. I hoped Chris was paying attention. My mind could only grasp small snatches of the conversation.

The very phrase "home for unwed mothers" had always evoked morbid fascination in me. It was the same intense but distanced awe the missionaries of the poor aroused as they preached kindness and charity to us—the straight-backed, square-shouldered men, stiffly coiffed wives, white-gloved, patent leather-shod daughters and crew-cut, freckle-faced sons, a congregation of "good" Catholic families. I could relate to being sent to a home for unwed mothers about as much as that righteous congregation could relate to the hungry bellies of the poor, as they tossed a few coins into the second collection of the day.

Our mugs chimed against the still half-full pitcher as we put them back on the table. Sarah's eyes caught mine as she got up to leave. I wished I could interpret their message. I looked up into Chris's eyes as he pulled the chair back for me. I saw all the love we had for each other, and all the strain he was under, too, etched there. It was still hard for me to believe that we weren't going to get married.

After the decision was made, I became like a child again to my parents. Mom took over and made the appointment with Catholic Social Services to work out arrangements for my entering Seton House, the home where Sarah had gone. She had driven me to our interview that morning. I had been a passenger in the car, a spectator at the interview.

Now, I realized the interview was over, the arrangements made. In three months I would be a resident of a home for unwed mothers. Sister was shaking my mother's hand, reassuring her that we were doing the right thing for the baby and for me. For a split second I thought my mother was going to genuflect and kiss Sister's hand in gratitude. I let myself go numb to deaden the pain.

I made it to our car. Mom got into the driver's seat and turned on the ignition. We were parked in the shade of a willow tree, but it was an oven inside anyway. She put her hand on the automatic gear shift knob and then stopped and turned to me. "No one is to know about your condition," she said. "It must be a complete secret, and that includes your friends, Jessica and Cindy." As if, on command, they could forget all they knew! And I was to start wearing girdles, though my stomach was still flat.

I didn't respond. I looked straight ahead at the willow tree as we pulled away from it.

———

It was difficult for Chris and me to see much of each other now, although we got together as much as we could. We still met at the Castle, but we were always afraid my parents would find out.

I kept my summer job at J.C. Penney's at the Friendly Shopping Center. One day my mother came home, laughing hysterically, tears streaming down her face. She seemed my age all of a sudden. A neighbor from across the street had stopped her that morning to remark on how *thin* I'd looked when I helped her at Penney's. It seemed that my A-line shifts perfectly concealed my embarrassing situation.

I was fortunate that fashions were not focussed on the waist that summer. In August I was to be maid of honor at my cousin Joanie's wedding. My dress arrived and I tried it on. I had had no idea of the tension my mother had been suppressing until I heard her guttural sigh of relief as the pink chiffon A-line skirt slid easily over my hips. We praised the Lord it was an Empire style. Still, there was a month to go before the wedding.

The morning of the wedding my cousin's house was packed with people. I was upstairs dressing when my mother came to check on my progress. The dress fit even though I was four months along.

The girdles she had packed for me to wear were still in the suitcase. When my mother spotted them in there and not on me, she had a fit. In a raging whisper she insisted I wear them, *both* of them. Her "whispers" were going to let the secret out far sooner than my not wearing them would. One was a long-line that extended from just below my bra almost to my knees. Since one of the garters was missing, the leg kept rolling up until it felt like a tourniquet around my thigh. Anyone touching me around the waist would have had to become suspicious. I could hardly breathe, hardly move in them, and I figured I might as well be wearing a scarlet *P*. But Mom stayed right by me as I put them on and did not leave my side until we arrived at the church.

Dappled light streamed through the stained glass windows of the church and fell on all of us like thousands of flower petals. We proceeded down the aisle. I was just ahead of Joanie, the bride. I felt graced to be her maid of honor. Under my bouquet, my hand rested lightly on my belly. I thought I felt a stirring inside. I looked up toward the altar and all at once I knew that I was at complete peace with God about my situation. I knew He wanted me there in His church as Joanie's maid of honor. However, I alternated between shame and barely controlled mirth as I wondered how the priest and all those assembled would react if they knew. I wondered how Mom had worked this one out with her beliefs.

Sure enough, it seemed that everyone had to touch my waist as they greeted me in the receiving line. I was sure that they would all wonder why I wore a long-line girdle with an Empire-style dress, especially as I was really thin. Joanie's new husband Tom introduced me as "John" out of sheer nervousness. His best man kept asking me, "John," to dance. My father was beside himself. My mother was a wreck even though everything was going well. But it seemed natural, not perverted, to enjoy Joanie's wedding, even though it was difficult not to wish it were my wedding.

School was to resume in mid-August, less than two weeks later. Everyone at home thought I was going back to school. Everyone at school thought I was spending a semester with a friend in Florida. Actually I was going to stay at my roommate's sister Tessa's apartment in Charlotte.

The lies and secrecy were wearing me out. My whole summer was one lie after another. Out-of-wedlock pregnancies were an intriguing topic of conversation, but never discussed except in whispers and innuendos. To the whole community, as well as my parents, secrecy was easier. I did not feel "unwed" or "out of wedlock." I felt pregnant with a baby for whom I already had a great deal of love. But I accepted the situation. This was how it was done.

I was beginning to really feel pregnant by the end of the summer. Reality hit home as my friends began to prepare to return to school, packing trunks with new clothes and new hopes. The A-line was losing its shape and becoming the sack, a shapeless style, distinguished by a dropped waist and voluminous folds around the midsection. In terms of fashion, I couldn't have chosen a better time to be in this situation.

I had to pretend to everyone that I was excited about beginning my sophomore year. And I was pretending to my parents that I was handling it all—the lies, my prospects—just fine. I often wondered if I were going mad. My heart felt heavy but I could not cry. I felt I had to be brave. I had put my faith in my parents and in the Church to know what was right. Certainly they had more wisdom than I, a nineteen-year-old. I attributed my hidden pain to my own madness. They would never put me through this if they knew I was feeling such agony.

Before leaving for Charlotte, I had to visit the doctor. My mother did not go with me. Two very pregnant women were sitting in the tiny reception area. I kept my left hand in my pocket so they wouldn't notice I had no wedding band. I felt raw with embarrassment and humiliation at having to hide my pregnancy. The two women, so full with their children, seemed to glow. I hoped they understood their good fortune. Just as the one across from me knitted a tiny baby sweater, I began to knit a cocoon to withdraw into. It was good that I had started on it then. During the examination the doctor seemed to treat me as if I had leprosy. I felt degraded by his lack of compassion. His only comment was that I had been pretty stupid to get into this fix. It was like he had spat on me, a poor beggar woman along a dusty road to Babylon. But at this point part of me didn't blame him.

I kept the blinds drawn at Tessa's apartment. Within two days of getting there I began to show a little. Tessa was sweet to me, like an older sister. She was a single working woman, a rare breed in those days when most women married right after they finished their schooling. It was fascinating being in the apartment of a woman on her own. But my shame kept me indoors. I didn't want to embarrass Tessa. I spent the days in limbo, with the TV on most of the time.

I could feel my baby kicking all the time now. As I sat through endless episodes of "Jeopardy" and the soaps, he grew to be my companion, and I held my hand on my belly most of the time to keep our connection. I had always been sociable and on the go constantly. This isolation was a tremendous reversal for me.

One weekend when Tessa was out of town, Chris drove for eight hours from his college to see me. The further along in my pregnancy I got, the more of a woman I became and the more absurd certain situations seemed. Why should I have to sneak around to see the father of my child? Yet I felt guilty. When Chris first walked into the apartment, I felt I was looking at him from far, far away, almost as if he were a stranger. It had been six weeks since we had been together. He was in his senior year. His life hadn't changed much, it seemed. The changes for me, inside and out, were like night and day.

I didn't know how I felt about seeing him again. Neither one of us had had even a moment's counseling; what we might be thinking and feeling was left to us to deal with. We were two babes in the woods alone in that Charlotte apartment. As we lay together that night, Chris put his hand on my belly and felt our baby move. Our awkwardness with each other went away and we were reconnected.

In the middle of October the call finally came. There was a space at Seton House. I thought for a second about the girl whose place I was about to take and her baby, now separated from each other. Panic rose up in me as I packed my things. I felt I was going to a foreign country, never to return.

Chapter Two

When I was four years old I had watched the sunlight create sparkling reflections on my new black patent Mary Janes and let the wind balloon under my yellow eyelet dress so I could punch it down, feeling like a princess, with my fresh green straw Easter bonnet, bound with velvet ribbon, perched on my long wavy blonde hair. I was sitting on the front seat of the car, with Daddy all to myself, as he drove me to the hospital to get my tonsils out. Then, I remember, came the cold steel frame of the operating table and the doctor who leaned over me and told me that, as soon as I had the injection, my tonsils would be out. That had made no sense to me, even at four. As they held the ether over my face, I panicked. I fought and called out for my father. But he wasn't there.

Now Dad was driving me to Seton House but it wasn't the wind that had created the balloon in my dress. The late afternoon sky was dark with thick cloud cover as we drove down Monument Avenue in Richmond. I looked up into the stone faces of the great Civil War heroes and felt a kind of reproach coming from them.

Seton House was on one of the main avenues, alongside office buildings, apartments, and a shopping center. There were big shade trees in front, but as far as I was concerned it was not hidden enough. I wondered if it aroused morbid curiosity in passing motorists. I wondered if little kids sneaked into the bushes to peek at it. I wondered if teenagers made it a regular haunt for tricks on Halloween or other occasions. (And did a young teenaged girl ever sit in silent compassion in the backseat as her companions hooted and hollered from their cruising car?)

I wondered if parents drove by and said a silent prayer to spare their daughters and themselves that pain and humiliation. Or said a prayer out loud in thanksgiving that their kids had made it through and were well on their way to fulfilling their parents' dreams. I could not believe that I would be living within the walls of such a place. I could not believe my father was really going to drive off and leave me there. But he did, even though I am sure his heart was ripped apart as he drove away.

There was only enough time for a quick tour of the facilities. Dinner would be served in a half hour. Sister Beatrice inclined her head toward the hall to indicate that the tour was beginning. I followed with trepidation, carrying my one small suitcase. I wouldn't need much in this place.

Gray light from the overcast sky filtered into the foyer. To the left of the entrance was the mother superior's office where the girls were admitted and where, I was informed, the adoptive parents would pick up their blessed bundle. With some bitterness, I thought, probably the sun will be shining for them.

I tried not to let impressions register too deeply, as I attempted to protect my heart and my baby from what was going on. Unfortunately, I didn't miss a thing.

Past the mother superior's office was the dining hall and to the right of the entrance was the chapel. I peered in and it was dark, with a faint trace of incense. The girls' rooms were all down one hall along one side of the building. Two large communal bathrooms with several shower stalls each, the laundry room, and a phone booth flanked the opposite side of the hall. At the end of the hall behind double doors was a large TV and recreation room. Chairs lined the walls. A large circular table stood in the far corner. As we turned back, Sister said that the nuns' quarters were in the left wing: the Mary Magdalenes on the right, the Virgin Marys on the left.

As I followed the tiny figure, I heard the deep rustle of her dark habit. The wood beads of her rosary marked the rhythm of her steady pace. She began to recite her litany of rules: We were not to run in the halls. We were not allowed in the TV room until after lunch. Mass was every morning at eight o'clock. The doctor came Thursday nights. Saturday was the day for wash and major chores. We were not allowed to miss any meals.

The most important rule, however, forbade us to tell anyone our last names, where we were from, or what schools we attended. No one was to know anything personal about any of the girls. A violation would be cause for immediate expulsion from Seton House. (Did they actually turn a pregnant girl out onto the street?) If we wanted to, we could make up a name or create a nickname.

That was an intriguing notion. I hadn't thought of changing

my name since sixth grade. Here was my opportunity to create a whole new persona. I had five minutes before dinner to come up with one before I was introduced to the other inmates.

Sister steered me into a plain room done in brownish greens and greenish browns. Over each bed hung a crucifix. My roommate was there waiting to meet me. She was petite, with long brown hair almost to her waist. There was a serious expression on her face. She had the bed by the window. Her due date was after mine so I gave up any hope of having that bed. She introduced herself as Anne-Marie. I wondered if that was her real name.

Sister stood framed by the doorway. Her skin was paper thin: transparent and ashen. Only nuns seemed to acquire such a deathly cast to their complexion. As we followed Sister down the hall, she asked if I had come up with a new name. Unfortunately, another one had eluded me; I was disappointed in my lack of imagination. Perhaps if I had been able to re-create my self at that instant, I might have had the power, as well, to struggle to keep my baby. But I could only accept—passively, guiltily—all that was told to me.

As I walked down the hall to the dining room, I felt my growing belly. My love flowed through my hands to my baby. In a strange way, I finally seemed safe. I could release the muscles that had helped hide my horrible secret. I could let myself be the expectant mother that I was. A peace came to me that I hadn't anticipated.

Yet, approaching the dining room, I was filled with foreboding. I had my own preconceived notions about what an "unwed mother" was like, despite the fact that I was one myself. I feared the girls in the dining room would be just one step above juvenile delinquents. For sure they would be wearing tons of makeup, their eyes black and dramatically drawn like those of

Egyptian harlots; Pan-Cake makeup would be slathered on thick to cover their bad complexions and their bleached hair ratted into enormous beehives that hadn't moved for two weeks. And all of them would be snapping gum in unison, and they would sneer when introduced to me.

Or else they would be dumb little country girls with used-up eyes and stringy dishwater blonde hair. Their boyfriends drove pickup trucks with rifles in the back window and they probably weren't sure who the father of their baby was. Their eyes would slide away from mine when we met. Or maybe they would be motorcycle molls, with silver-studded black-leather maternity tops, their black hair greased back into DAs to match their boyfriends'. They would stare me up and down and then they would all laugh hysterically and turn away from me.

Heat from the adjacent kitchen warmed up the dining room and escaped past me as I opened the door. Light flooded the room from overhead fluorescent lights. There was lots of chatter amidst the clinking of silverware and the clattering of pots and pans in the kitchen. It all became silent as I was briefly introduced by my first name.

The faces, turned up at me, all seemed pretty normal. It could have been our college cafeteria except for the big bellies. I sat down timidly next to my roommate and she introduced me to the others at our end of the table—first names only. Immediately, I began to get the scoop about the sisters and Seton House. But we were all careful about revealing anything that might identify us. It was quite a trick to get acquainted with someone under these rules. The youngest girl was fifteen, the oldest twenty-three. Mostly we were nineteen or twenty years old.

Six of the girls were planning an outing on Saturday to the nearby coffee shop and then the shopping center. Lunch was to

the dresser cast a golden glow in the room and on me. I looked at myself in wonder, so full of my baby. I wished Chris could see me.

By afternoon on New Year's Day, it was clear that Pamela was in labor. I had guessed, as she had been extremely quiet all day. But Pamela was usually pretty quiet. Since she had apparently been treated like a doll all her life, she did not know how to speak for herself. Her parents and her boyfriend waited somewhere far away for the error to be corrected, the unplanned baby born and disposed of. I wanted to get angry for her, but it would have been futile.

She suddenly let out a scream. Mrs. Hogan rushed over to her and motioned for us to stay back. Someone hurried down the hall for Sister Beatrice. I looked at Pamela's face. It seemed like she had finally woken up.

Sunday she delivered a boy. She had asked to be completely knocked out for the delivery and chose not to see her baby. She was the first one I had known to choose that option.

At Mass that morning, I tried to figure out what to pray for. I was almost a week overdue, at least by my calculations. Perhaps I had figured wrong. Or, perhaps, my child and I were trying to be together as long as we could. I was praying more to get out of this place than anything else. Chris was already back at school, beginning his last semester.

Each morning at breakfast, Nora and I looked for each other. We had the same due date. We just shook our heads, wondering when we would begin labor, not in control of a thing. The longer my baby waited to be born, the less chance I had. The ninth of January was the fork in the road for me. Either I got back to school in time, or I would be lost. The closer the day came, the closer I came to panic.

On Thursday afternoon, Nora and I sat together as we

watched the soaps. That night was Dr. Mandel's weekly visit, and we could both expect some sort of news after our examinations. Nora said she was going to ask him to try to induce her labor by starting her dilation. I didn't know that was possible, but I thought I would ask him about it for myself. Sunday would be January 9.

I lay back on the examining table, feet propped high in the stirrups, still trying hard to keep some semblance of dignity. Sister Beatrice was at my left shoulder holding the examining instruments for Dr. Mandel. He was too handsome for this job. He looked like Prince Charming. He and Father O'Brien were the only men we ever saw in this place. Dr. Mandel looked up, snapping off the rubber gloves. The cervix had softened some. He had tried to start dilation, but he could not guarantee that it would speed things up. He thought it could be another week at the most. I had lost four pounds that week, and that was his major concern. I had been eating everything and couldn't account for the weight loss. All my vital signs were normal. He was concerned I was feeling too much stress, but I didn't know how to control that.

Nora and I decided to try to go for a hike the next day, to encourage our babies a little. We woke up to a balmy spring day—in January. I didn't know where all the sunshine had come from. The weather was so beautiful, five of the others decided to join us. We made plans to go after lunch. But by eleven, Nora was already in labor. The rest of us decided to venture anyway.

The area behind Seton House was wooded, mostly with pine trees. There were a couple of paths. One led to the cow pasture at the edge of the Seton House property. Inspired by the great weather, we decided to head for the pasture. Once we broke away from the force field of Seton House, we felt practically like wood nymphs. We laughed at the incongruity of our bulky bodies as we climbed over fallen logs along the path. Sunlight speckled the evergreens, and they gave off their potent aroma as a balm. A thick carpet of dead leaves and pine needles kept the mud from oozing into our shoes.

At the end of the path was a barbed-wire fence that prevented the cows from wandering into our woods. In a spirit of delicious rebellion, a few of us decided to climb the fence into forbidden territory. No cows were in sight and the meadow was beautiful. The barbed-wire fence tore my dress in two places, but it didn't matter. Suddenly, I was free. The sun poured down on the open pasture. There was space in which to run free. I had forgotten what open space felt like.

We were boldly crossing the pasture when one of the girls, who had stayed back behind the fence, screamed. We turned around and stood facing the most enormous bull, approaching us with his girlfriends right behind him. The look in his eye indicated he was not fooling around. With split-second calculation, we ran as fast as we could for the fence. We each tore something trying to get through the fence quickly. We were laughing so hard we were practically sick. We turned back and saw the bull approaching at leisure, almost swaggering in the knowledge of his own power. Looking boldly back at him from behind the safety of the barbed wire, Anne-Marie cracked that he certainly seemed the quintessential male.

The sun fell behind a stand of trees in the late afternoon and a damp, cool blanket of air enveloped us, as we tramped back through the soggy leaves. I began to worry that I had hurt my baby during the escape from the bull. Could his head have banged up against my pelvic bone and caused serious injury? I would have thought he would be active after the jostling I'd given him. Instead, he was silent and eerily still. I became still, too, listening for any sign of life from him.

After the fresh air, the air inside Seton House seemed stale. Nora had already left for the hospital. I wondered if I would be here until Easter.

The next morning, I opened my eyes slowly, not wanting to move a muscle until I could get a sense if my baby was in danger. There was only the same absolute stillness. After breakfast, I found Sister Beatrice and told her my fears. Her face didn't reveal any concern as I followed her down to the infirmary. She said a baby does become silent a few days before birth. In the infirmary, she placed the icy cold stethoscope on my belly and located my baby's heartbeat. Everything seemed fine. Thank God.

That afternoon, I found I was the only one left. The others had gone for a Saturday outing. As I aimlessly wandered around the recreation room, I picked up the January issue of *Seventeen* magazine and stared back at a shining coed, smiling in bubbly innocence. I let the magazine slip through my fingers, and it landed with a loud smack on the table. It was so quiet. The sisters must have gone out, too. I picked up the ski sweater I had been knitting; I had finally come close to finishing. For a while it had been difficult to look at, after I realized, too late, that I had missed one stitch and the entire pattern was off. All those stitches, and one wrong one had ruined the whole design.

Through the haze of my afternoon nap, I heard the girls returning. It had been a dreamless nap. I felt like nothing since my baby had stopped moving. Without his company I felt abandoned, lifeless. Thankfully, after their outing, there would be lots of stories and purchases to examine and forbidden food smuggled in. I would be distracted from the afternoon's emptiness. Anne-Marie came in with news that Nora had delivered a daughter.

At dinner, I had one letter; it was from Chris. I slipped it into my pocket, and saved it to read before going to sleep.

I sat on the edge of my bed, in the soft light from the dresser lamp, and read Chris's letter. I felt his anguish as I read between the lines. He was worried about my being late. His feelings of helplessness broke through the usual uplifting, encouraging tone of his letters. He, too, carried his emotional burden alone.

I turned out the light, lay down on my bed, and propped up my belly with a pillow. Our baby was still sleeping peacefully. I held Chris's letter close to my heart. I could almost feel him lying there, arms around us, the three of us together as we should have been. I drifted into a deep, deep sleep.

Sunday, January 9, 1966. My eyes opened wide at first light. I had slept so soundly, I had not moved the whole night. This was the day my baby would be born. Somehow I knew. I pulled the blanket from my bed and wrapped myself up against the early morning chill, then padded down the hall to the recreation room. I sat down in one of the chairs, like an old Indian grandmother. The room was filled with a heavy grayness. I sat in a sort of vacant suspension, yet I was acutely aware of the tiniest details in the room. There were still two hours left before everyone would be getting up. Nothing seemed to matter but my all-encompassing awareness. The first contraction gripped my belly, and a tear slid down my cheek. I had to begin saying goodbye.

As I stared at the empty television screen, I thought back over all the moments we had had together. I felt wrapped in a cocoon, completely alone, yet attended by unseen angelic midwives. I felt regal, as if I were in another time and place, as well as there at Seton House.

Another contraction came like a wave. The contractions originated in my lower back. The pain seemed to begin at a point close to the base of my spine and fan out from there. My sides tightened hard, but the contractions were not able to meet at the center of my belly. Though they were not what I had been told to anticipate, I knew they were real.

The first slam of the bathroom door, as the girls began stirring, startled me. Two hours had somehow passed. The light in the room had become clear and bright, the colors vivid. After the latest contraction subsided, I pulled myself up out of the chair and let the blanket fall off my shoulders. With care, I made my way down the hall to my room. I knew I couldn't sit through Mass. But the contractions were quite manageable still, so I decided to keep this secret to myself a little longer.

I stood under the shower, letting the water pour over my belly as I shampooed my hair. Leaning over to shave my legs was difficult. But I was determined not to have hairy legs at so great a moment as my baby's birth. The water turned cold before I finally finished. If the sisters knew what I was up to, they would have been quite upset.

After drying my hair and putting on fresh clothes, I went to the phone booth to try to call Chris. There was no answer. I decided not to call home until after I delivered. I didn't want to worry about my parents worrying about me. I needed my strength for myself.

On the way back to my room from the phone, the first really big contraction gripped me. The pain shot from my back down my legs. I had to hold onto the wall. I decided it was best to go back to bed.

I propped myself up with a book and a clock. The contractions were still coming from my back. Maybe this was not labor after all. That was supposed to harden the abdominal muscles. Yet, whatever it was, it was coming five minutes apart. I read for a while as I timed the contractions, and then drifted into a light sleep.

A sharp contraction woke me up, and I muffled a little cry. I looked over to the window, and saw Anne-Marie sitting on the edge of her mattress, watching over me. I felt a kinship to her now. She said she had suspected that I was in labor when she saw me sitting alone in the recreation room. She asked if she should call Sister Beatrice, and I begged her to wait.

By three o'clock, my unusual contractions were coming three minutes apart. I asked Anne-Marie to call Sister Beatrice. The rustle of her billowing habit announced her arrival. She seemed quite efficient as she sat on the edge of my bed, hand on my belly, waiting for my next contraction to come. It took an interminable time. It was almost as if she had frightened it away. She was about to stand up and leave when I felt a strong one. The pain was so strong I had to dig my heels into the mattress to cope. She looked down at me, her hand on my belly, and said she didn't feel anything. Her brow furrowed into a dramatic expression of grave doubt. I was aghast. At this point, I had no doubts. I was angry. How could she stand there and tell me I was not in labor, when I knew damn well I was? How could I believe her rather than my own body? To humor me, she hung around for another contraction. That one was nine minutes coming. Again, though the pain in my back was quite intense, my belly was as soft as a powder puff.

The cross from her rosary swung wildly from side to side as she got up to leave the room. The swoosh of her habit created a breeze on my face. As Sister's footsteps disappeared down the hall, I told Anne-Marie she might end up delivering my baby if

Sister Beatrice didn't change her mind. The pain in my back grew in intensity. With each contraction, my heels dug deeper grooves into the mattress. The radius of the pain now extended up my back, but my belly never hardened.

At four-thirty, when the pains were two minutes apart, I asked Anne-Marie to please get Sister Beatrice. She came bustling back, clearly skeptical. Again, she could not feel the contraction. She shook her head in what looked like pity to me. Then my heels began digging furiously again after less than two minutes, and she paid attention. She asked Anne-Marie to find Sister Agatha to get her opinion. I prayed they didn't take too long.

Sister Agatha hurried in. She asked Anne-Marie for a history of the alleged labor. Why didn't she ask me? What did I have to do to convince these two nuns that I was not only in labor, but my baby would come tonight?

At five o'clock, though not at all convinced, they called the doctor and decided to send me to the hospital. I asked Anne-Marie to please call Chris. As the girls helped me down the hall, Sister Beatrice told them I would probably be returning tonight.

The air was shockingly cold on my face when the ambulance attendants split open the double doors with their stretcher. I looked at Sister Beatrice in panicky protest. I had no idea that we were taken by ambulance to the hospital. But I had no say in the matter. The attendants stood on either side of me. Sister watched them lift me up onto the stretcher and strap me down. I could feel myself beginning to hyperventilate from claustrophobia and indignation and mortification. I couldn't understand the need for this. I wasn't sick or dying or crazy. Not yet.

They wheeled me through the doors into the cold night air, right in the midst of one of my contractions. The name Lakeside Volunteer Rescue Squad was emblazoned in big red letters along the side of the white ambulance. They wheeled the stretcher up the ramp. One of the attendants hopped in alongside me, and the driver slammed the doors shut. We sped into the dark night.

The interior of the vehicle was dimly lit. The little light there was danced off the chrome trim and steel instruments. I looked up into the attendant's eyes. They looked down on me with much more sympathy and compassion than I had seen in a very long time. But I was still in shock at being alone, strapped down on a stretcher in a careening ambulance with two strange men, in the most vulnerable state a woman could be in. Then the attendant reached up to the ceiling and switched on the siren. Absolute horror took hold of me. After all the furtive secrecy—the tension my mother lived with day after day, racing to be the first at the mailbox; the exciting stories I had concocted about my school life for hometown correspondents, about the wonderful Florida beaches for my college friends, the incredible number of lies that had been and were being told to keep my pregnancy a secret—this man turned on the siren and announced it to the whole world. I began to laugh hysterically and the attendant laughed with me. I asked him, nevertheless, to please turn it off. I had never heard anything so loud. He said he couldn't, to sit back and enjoy the ride.

As the ambulance turned into the brightly lit emergency entrance, he finally turned it off and held my strapped-down arm through one of my contractions. The driver jumped out of his seat and ran around to open the back doors. Together they wheeled me off and up a ramp into the emergency room. The stretcher came to a stop in the middle of the room. To my left sat an old black man, hat in hand, eyes red and watery, looking exhausted and dejected. To my right, doctors and nurses were scurrying in and out of the treatment rooms, busy and bright.

At my head stood my two attendants, patiently waiting for a nurse to come claim me. The bright lights were glaring after three months of subdued lighting at Seton House, where we were always turning off lights to conserve electricity.

As I lay on the stretcher, I prayed to get out of such a public place, before everyone in the hospital read the bright red neon sign flashing over my body, proclaiming me one of those Seton House girls. The pain of public humiliation was much worse than my labor at that point.

A strawberry-blonde nurse broke away from the bustling crowd of patients and healers, and, scanning me, lifted her face to the attendants in a silent question. They nodded yes, confirming that I was the one. I watched, feeling as powerless as a rag doll. Where were they going to toss me next? The attendant, who had been by my side during the ride, advised the nurse that they would wait, as Sister had felt I was not actually in labor. The nurse, noticing the pain washing over my face, reached over and felt my lower belly. "Wheel her up to Maternity immediately," she commanded two orderlies.

Up I went in the oversized hospital elevator with two more strangers. The elevator doors rumbled open. Tears stung my eyes, but I could not wipe them away: my arms were strapped down. My stretcher was wheeled alongside a hospital bed in the labor room. The orderlies undid the straps, and, reaching under me, deftly lifted me over onto the bed. Then they wheeled the stretcher away.

In the bed next to me, only a few feet away, a woman began a low moan of pain that built higher and higher to a crescendo of screams and obscenities, then subsided into mumbled, angry complaints. The strawberry-blonde nurse from Emergency had come up to check that I arrived where I was supposed to. She noticed my look of alarm at my new companion and assured me that the woman would be delivering soon. She slid the curtain between us closed, patted me on the shoulder, and said a nurse would be with me in a little while.

Within minutes, another nurse came and gave me a quick exam. I was already five centimeters dilated. Then another nurse joined her, and together they prepped me, not even stopping to allow me to have a contraction. I believed they would have been more courteous to the woman next to me, since her husband was in the waiting room, and she was there legitimately. Then, the nurses opened the curtain. I couldn't help staring at the woman on the next bed. I was fascinated by her ability to let all her feelings out with no inhibitions. I vowed I would not cry out. I would show them that, though I was from Seton House, I still had some self-respect.

In a short while, a tall, distinguished-looking doctor walked in. His presence cleared a path toward the screaming woman. The curtain was quickly drawn again, and then, just as quickly, she was wheeled off to the delivery room.

I was now the only woman in labor in the labor room. Two of the nurses wheeled my bed down a hall and parked me up against a mustard-yellow wall across from their coffee room. I felt like a little child parked in a playpen. Again I thought, they would not have taken such liberties with the married woman. The clock above the refrigerator in the coffee room said 6:45. The nurses sat down at the Formica table and proceeded to play cards. I lay on my back, knees propped up, and at each contraction, I rolled over and faced the mustard-yellow wall, gripping the steel rail of the bed. It was such a horrible color. As each contraction subsided, I'd uncurl from the fetal position I had assumed and watch the nurses as they played gin rummy. They never looked up from their cards. Just as one was about to lay down her hand, I let out a cry that surprised me. I heard the cards being slapped down quickly on the table, as they rushed over to me. Without asking a question, they wheeled me back to the labor room.

As one stayed with me, another ran to the nurses' station to call Dr. Jordan. It was eight-thirty. I was eight centimeters dilated. The pain in my back was severe. It felt like my spine would break in two or fracture into millions of pieces. If it hurt this much for me, I couldn't imagine what it must be like for my baby. The nurse came back with news that Dr. Jordan had gone to dinner with his family, and had not left a number, assuming from Sister Beatrice's report that I would not deliver any time soon. Without his okay, I could not be given an epidural. He was not expected back for some time. I wondered if I could last without fainting. I kept apologizing for not being able to handle the pain better. They reassured me that I was actually being quite brave.

At nine o'clock I was fully dilated. I saw the grave concern on the nurse's face as the other one ran again to try to find Dr. Jordan. She rushed back. No luck. The head nurse asked that Dr. West, the anesthesiologist, get everything set up, to be ready the minute they heard from Dr. Jordan.

I heard the wheels of the cart clicking over the edges of the linoleum blocks. Then Dr. West was showing me the long needle that would be inserted in my spine, the conduit for the painkiller. Because the labor was in my back, they didn't want to use a caudal. The nurse announced the baby's head was crowning. A thrill ran through me. She told Dr. West to go ahead. He warned me not to move a muscle, no matter how hard the contraction. If he missed, it would cause serious injury. The liquid entered the base of my spine, and spread like a sickening heat until numbness took over. I hated the feeling and began to panic. I wanted to feel my baby being born. They asked me if I wanted a drug that would put me out and I said no way. They gave me a sedative, much stronger than I had expected, which dulled my emotions and my mind. I fought through a haze to keep alert to what was happening.

The nurse had sent for all the equipment she would need to deliver my baby right on the spot. That would have been fine. I trusted her, and I could tell she cared about what happened. I could feel how close I was to giving birth. I was really thrilled.

Then from down the hall, a voice announced that Dr. Jordan had arrived. His presence obliterated the camaraderie and gaiety of our shared drama. He took command and ordered me sent to the delivery room immediately. Without ever looking at me, he walked away to scrub. In subdued silence, the nurses prepared me for delivery. They put me in a fresh gown, then transferred me to a gurney with great care not to dislodge the needle. The narrowness of the gurney made me feel insecure. The freshness of the sheets seemed harsh. Everything was changing rapidly, out of my control.

The end of the gurney parted the doors into the delivery room. The nurse who had been with me, who had made me feel safe, could not stay. With an encouraging pat on my shoulder, she transferred me over to the delivery room nurse. This woman was totally unsympathetic. Under her dyed black hair, her face held no trace of humor. She never looked straight at me. She frightened me. She and Dr. West transferred me from the gurney to the delivery room table. She strapped my legs high up in the stirrups, and then strapped my arms down by my side. I was in shackles, unable to move. She still had said nothing to me and I was too terrified to speak to her. The anesthetic dulled my panic a little. I looked up into Dr. West's eyes. He no longer cracked jokes to keep my spirits up. I asked him to cut back more on the medicine. I could tell he felt very sorry for me. It was difficult to feel the joy of giving birth in such an atmosphere.

The nurse stood at attention to my left, waiting for Dr. Jordan to take over. She had done her work. Dr. West waited quietly to my right, by my head, out of my vision. I wished I could see him more easily. I needed someone there who would make me feel safe. It was a small room, glaring in its stark whiteness. The powerful overhead lights illuminated without mercy. Our discomfort with each other was mutual.

Dr. Jordan finally strolled in. With detached efficiency, he took his position between my immodestly splayed legs. I wanted my arms free of the straps, so I could hold my hands on my belly and send love and strength to my baby in his last heroic efforts. The nurse told me not to move, because of the epidural needle. Numbed and fettered, I was stripped of all my capacity to help my baby be born.

There was a tiny mirror behind the doctor through which I could watch the birth. The doctor's body blocked my vision. At first I thought his position was necessary. But then I realized he did not care whether or not I saw. I asked him, timidly, if he could please stand aside, so I could see. Without comment, but with a look of annoyance, he shifted his position a little. I could see now, but I had to strain. It didn't matter. Nothing they did could take this moment from me. It was mine and my baby's.

I could see the crown of my baby's head. I was swept away by the miracle of it. Slowly and carefully, Dr. Jordan's gloved hands, glistening with the blood and mucus of my body, grasped my baby's head and began to pull him out as I gave one final push. I watched in amazement as my belly collapsed and became suddenly empty. It was 9:51 P.M.

Dr. Jordan held the baby straight up by his tiny feet. In the joy of the moment, he forgot the circumstances of this little being's birth. He welcomed my baby to the world, and acknowledged my motherhood. "You have a son," he smiled down at me. "He is a very pretty baby."

I wanted to hold my baby's tiny naked body, just as it was, as it came from mine. But my arms were still strapped down. I never had felt such a longing, as I watched them put drops in his eyes, wash and weigh him. I wanted my baby. This sudden separation was too horrible a shock. I watched their every move.

He weighed six pounds ten ounces, and was nineteen inches long. He had all his fingers and toes and was perfect. The nurse swaddled him and laid him down in the clear plastic bassinet beside me. I asked her to please let me hold him. She seemed surprised by my request and uncertain about whether to grant it. Something she saw in my eyes must have convinced her she had better. She had to come around to my other side to undo the straps on my arms so I could hold him. I never took my eyes off him. He was so beautiful. Finally, my arms were free. I asked her to free my baby's hands from the swaddling blanket, too, so I could see them and touch them with my own. She was annoyed. I did not care.

My hands caressed my son's tiny body, feeling his limbs through the soft warm flannel. Only yesterday, I had felt them through my own skin. His sweetness was overwhelming. He looked like a little Indian, black hair poking out from the swaddling blanket. My uterus contracted in longing for him. My breasts began to swell, wanting to nourish him. My heart encircled us and, for a moment, we were the only two in the room.

Then the nurse lifted him from my arms. I knew to expect this, from our classes at Seton House. It was standard procedure to take the babies to the nursery to monitor their vital signs. What had seemed logical in the class, seemed like an atrocity now. I had no choice but to watch them take him away.

Only after his bassinet disappeared did I tune into what was happening to my body. Dr. Jordan was stitching up the episiotomy. I could feel the tug of his needlework, but I didn't feel any pain. Suddenly, I felt drained, overwhelmed. Dr. West was explaining that he was giving me a shot to keep my breasts from producing milk. There was no place left in which the impact of those words could register in my conscious mind, but my body reacted with sudden nausea.

I was wheeled into the darkened, four-bed recovery room. As I entered, the woman who had labored next to me was wheeled out. She was only semiconscious, still heavily sedated. I was given two Darvon and told to try to sleep. I was instructed not to get out of the bed without first ringing for the nurse to assist. There was one tiny light over the sink in the far end of the room. I stared at it, fighting tears and loneliness. At some point, I fell asleep. At some point later in the night, I was transferred to another room.

Chapter Five

A nurse opened the blinds to the tall window in my room. Sunshine poured onto an empty bed next to the window, and I sighed in relief. I had not wanted to share a room. It would have been too embarrassing to have to make up a story to explain why I was all alone, without visitors. I also didn't believe it would be easy for me to watch a woman with her new baby, surrounded by husband and family.

The nursery felt a thousand miles away. I asked the nurse how my baby was doing. She said he was doing very well and had slept soundly. She shifted a bit in discomfort as she stood at the door, as if she wanted to leave. When could I see him? She said she didn't know if I was allowed to. My God, he was *my* baby. He hadn't been adopted yet. I told her that it had been arranged for me to feed my baby while I was here. She said, if that was true, then they would bring him in at nine o'clock, after breakfast and early morning rounds.

The aroma of bacon and eggs reached my room before the tray did. I had heard the nurse's aide as she made her way down the hall with bubbly questions for all the other new mothers. She passed my breakfast tray to me without a word or a smile. I began to feel self-conscious. It was the sort of discomfort a thirteen-year-old would feel when all her peers were treating her cruelly, laughing about her behind her back, but not admitting their animosity, making her doubly unsure. It made me want to get out of there, to go back to Seton House where they at least accepted me. Except my baby was here, and I had to be with him as long as possible. My body ached for him.

I called Chris. He had skipped classes to wait for my call. Anne-Marie had phoned him the night before to tell him of our son. He and Ted were going to drive up to see me. He didn't care how much trouble he got into. They would find a way of sneaking into my room. After all the months of confinement and fear of breaking the rules, I almost balked. But we had to see each other, whether or not anyone else in this world consented.

I knew I had to call home next. My parents would naturally want to know it was all over. I braced myself as I dialed. Telling my parents about their first grandchild, I wanted to be able to announce it as joyous news. Mom answered. It was a boy, I said. There was silence at the other end, as if she was shocked at my news. Had they convinced themselves I wasn't going to give birth to anything?

Sister Dominic had told us we would all forget. Were they afraid that this information might jeopardize their ability to forget? I was only able to imagine what they were thinking. We didn't talk about feelings. Mom didn't ask anything about my labor or delivery or how I felt. Her only question was when could I come home. Friday, I said. They would be there first thing Friday, she promised, as if these were the magical words that would make everything okay again. I felt despondent as I hung up the phone.

Then I heard the little babies' cries coming down the hall. I came out of my reverie at once. My breasts swelled and leaked little drops of milk in anticipation of seeing my son. I figured out, by the sounds, that my room was the last one down the hall. I strained to hear the clickity-click of my son's bassinet wheels as they rolled him to me. At long last he was wheeled in. The nurse gathered him up and handed him to me. My heart nearly burst. He was in the deepest, most peaceful sleep I had ever seen. His face held celestial serenity. His tiny body felt solid and surprisingly strong. His warmth floated up to me, like the smell of sweet jasmine. He was swaddled like a mummy in his soft little blue flannel blanket and fit perfectly in the nook of my arm, up next to my heart. I looked down at his blissful face and I wanted him to wake up and be with me. We had so little time to be together.

The nurse handed me a warm bottle of sugar water. I realized she knew I was a Seton House girl, because she didn't bother to teach me anything about his care. All the little, seemingly insignificant, unspoken messages were coming in loud and clear. But as I looked down at my sleeping baby, his peace washed over me as well. I tasted a little drop of the sugar water off the tip of my finger. It was quite sweet. I outlined his mouth with the nipple, moistening it a little. A wise and mischievous smile began at the corner of his mouth and spread to light up his face. His eyes were still closed. His smile seemed to come from a faraway memory. Such a brilliant child, to smile his first day. Milk filled my breasts again, suddenly, and took me by surprise. I wanted to try to nurse him, but I felt I had no right, that if they caught me, they might not bring him back to me. They had already succeeded in convincing me that I was not entitled to him. They might allow me the privilege of holding him, but he was not mine.

I hazily remembered that I had been given a shot to stop my milk. The shot might poison my milk and hurt my baby. So I strangled my impulse to put him to nurse at my breast. I began to wonder if, indeed, he would be better off without me. I was not good enough for him. When I heard the clicking sound of the bassinet wheels begin again, my heart sank. They came straight to me first. I told the nurse I didn't think it was fair that I should get him last, and then have him taken first. She said the other mothers needed a little extra time to get used to their babies, before they took them home. When she took my baby out of my arms, it felt like she pulled my heart out with him.

I spent the time awaiting his next visit deciding on a name to give him. I wanted to get to know him first to be certain it was the right one for him, but I also wanted to call him by name as quickly as I could. I narrowed the choice to Phillip or Paul for no reason, except that I liked both names. But then I thought he should have Chris's name, since my last name would be on his birth certificate. Then we would both be with him somehow.

"Phillip" sounded the best when I said the whole name out loud. "Phillip Christopher." "Phillip" had strength, a regal quality, yet sounded gentle and sensitive. It could be the name of an artist. I wished all those things for him. Now that I had named him, I had only to wait for him to be brought back to me again.

The starched hospital sheets chafed my skin a bit. I looked across the room at the white linoleum block floor, the empty bed, and the huge window. I could hear the nurses bustling in and out of the other mothers' rooms down the hall, chatting happily. No one was coming into my room. Feeling isolated, unable to know how to ask for help—and afraid I might not get it if I did—I sat propped up by the starched unyielding pillows. Their plastic covers crackled with each slight movement. The time seemed interminable.

Then there was a knock on my partially opened door and a young brunette with a long page-boy hairdo stuck her head in and looked about searching for me. I was sitting on the edge of the bed, about to try to go across the hall to the bathroom. I did not have my robe on. I wore only the thin hospital gown.

She said hello brightly, as if we were meeting at a garden party. "Do you mind if we come in?" she asked, letting herself in without waiting for my reply. Behind her followed two men. The three of them wore street clothes. She clutched a clipboard to her breast as she introduced herself as a social worker. I didn't catch who the two men with her were. The three of them stood close to me, hovering. I felt naked and vulnerable in my thin gown. She only needed a moment of my time, she said briskly. But they needed my signature to authorize the hospital to take care of my son. It was a formality, she said.

I wished I had someone there to advise me about what I was signing. I hadn't had to sign anything legal in my life before. I asked if it was something permanent. She said no, but it was best if I signed it. She asked me to write in my child's name, if I had given him one, and then sign at the bottom. I felt I had no choice. I signed. They disappeared the moment I complied.

At one o'clock, I could hear the clickity-clack of the bassinet wheels and the "oohs" and "ahs" begin again. And then there was silence for a long time. My baby wasn't brought to me. I buzzed the nurses' station. The shift had changed. An older nurse with a stern face briskly walked into the room. I asked her where my baby was, afraid perhaps something was wrong with him. She reacted with surprise. Wasn't I a Seton House girl? Yes, I said, but I had made arrangements to feed my baby while I was in the hospital. She balked, but relented, bustling back out into the hall. Ten minutes later, she came back with my son. She put him in my arms with a grimace, as if she hated contaminating such a helpless infant. She said I had five minutes. He had already been fed. I was afraid to get her too angry with me by insisting on more time, in case they really did decide to forbid me to see him again.

I held him close. In exactly five minutes, the nurse came bustling back and unceremoniously emptied my arms. Again, my body ached for him. Each time they took him, more of me left with him. Not one person, not Sister Dominic or the Seton House sisters or even my own mother, had prepared me for feeling this.

Since I would be doing the best, most loving thing for my baby by giving him to good parents, I was supposed to be happy. The joy I would feel about doing the right thing was supposed to drown out any attachment feelings I might have. This sacrifice was really a blessing, my opportunity to regain the character I had lost by becoming pregnant in the first place. This sort of "robbing Peter to pay Paul" system of morality had been diligently instilled in me since my first catechism class. If one committed a sin, one did penance to wipe the slate clean again. Making love before the sacrament of marriage had been received, not to mention having a baby out of wedlock, was a mortal sin right up there with murder. Giving up the baby born of my most grievous sin was a wholly justified penance in the Church's eyes, and the only hope I had to reinstate myself in

God's grace and work my way back to a chance for heaven. I didn't believe all that now but I was in sufficient awe of the power of the Church to doubt my own feelings, my own instincts.

After a quick check down the hall, I scurried back across to my room from the bathroom where I had just showered. My physical vitality was strong. The stitches didn't bother me. My belly was flat already, since I had gained so little weight during the pregnancy. I was actually thinner than normal for me. I was eagerly anticipating Chris's visit.

I closed the blinds and turned on the light by my bed. The room felt cozy, like a nest. I climbed back into bed and succumbed to an illusion of bliss. I received my baby for his evening feeding and I whispered in his tiny ear that his father was coming to visit us. We would be coming down to the nursery to see him, so I asked him please to manage to have his eyes open. I told him his father was proud of him. I was caught up in my fantasy of a happy family and I hardly stirred when they took him from me. We were one after all, and never apart really.

I floated for another half hour in my transcendental state. Then from down the hall, I heard male voices and lots of chatter. Visiting hours were starting. Chris would be arriving soon. I stepped out of the room to cross the hall to the bathroom with my toothbrush already in my mouth. My heart stopped still, and my legs went weak from the shock. I was face-to-face with Chris. My toothbrush nearly poked him in the chin. He looked tremendously relieved to see me. He had been afraid to ask for my room number for fear of getting caught and simply had faith that he would find me. I told him to wait in my room, while I made a quick trip to the bathroom. I waved to Ted, who was hiding behind a huge rubber plant in the reception area. He waved back quickly but seemed eager to return to the safety of his rubber plant. We had no idea what, if anything, would happen if they were caught.

I was full of myself as a woman when I walked back into my room and sat on the bed next to Chris. As we talked about our baby, I realized the depth of love I had become capable of, love that we shared for each other. I thought I saw the same realization dawning in Chris's eyes.

But I was overwhelmed by doubts once again. I was a sinner, a fool. Chris didn't really love me. How could he? My parents would be ashamed, the sisters would be appalled. And the doctors and nurses were going to come in and arrest Chris for the scandal we were creating in the hospital. How could we flaunt ourselves in the face of all we had sinned against? How could we show our love for this baby by beginning his life in shame? We had made a mistake, and now we *had* to pay.

I wanted to get out of the room, quickly. I took Chris's hand, and we walked together down the hall to the nursery. The hall was dim but the nursery window illuminated the crowd of happy faces "oohing" and "aahing" over their tiny new babies. Chris and I eased ourselves into an opening at the corner of the glass. I searched all the little faces but I didn't find our baby. Then I saw him.

He was lying in his clear plastic bassinet, placed up against the back wall of the nursery, set apart from the others. His little head was turned away from us, facing the wall. They had him bundled and lying on his left side. I was surprised he could sleep in that position. He was twenty-five feet away. All we could see was his dark hair.

We tapped on the nursery window discreetly. The nurse

inside ignored us. I recognized her. She was the one from early afternoon. Chris tapped again, more insistently. We were embarrassed at having to draw attention to ourselves. Frowning, the nurse opened the nursery door, just wide enough to poke her face through to see what we wanted. I explained to her that Chris was my baby's father. Could she please swing the bassinet over to the window, so he could see his son? She shook her head no, and closed the door.

I couldn't believe it. Chris looked stunned. We knocked on the door again. The same nurse opened it, and in an impatient whisper told us that Seton House babies were not allowed to be brought to the window. Then she shut the door.

We leaned up close to the window, helpless in disbelief, and stared at our baby up against that wall. Then the nurse walked back over and closed the nursery curtains.

It was difficult for us to move away from the window. We were both too sad to speak.

Back in my room, Chris said we had to get married.

My brain seemed to split into two distinct halves. One side knew we could make it. It wouldn't be easy, and it wouldn't be the stuff of dreams, but it would be beautiful, because it was the right thing to do. The other half of my brain seemed clogged with the opinions and voices of everyone but me, saying it was impossible, selfish, wrong.

I was unable to look straight into his eyes. Instead I stared down at his hand holding mine. "If we got married after he was born, he would always be called a bastard. He would hate us," I said. "Bastard" was a word of mythological proportions then. I told Chris we should both think it through and talk about it with our parents. Visiting hours had ended ten minutes before, and the nurse might discover that he was still with me. It was almost impossible to let him go. We could hear the nurses making their evening rounds, dispensing medication. I looked out into the hall to see when the coast was clear. Ted was still sitting nervously behind the rubber plant. Chris motioned for him to follow. Then they waved and disappeared.

Closing the door behind me, I felt the coziness of my room had vanished. I went over to the window to see if I could catch a glimpse of them leaving, but the window did not afford a view of the parking lot. I climbed back into my bed and pulled the blankets up to my chin. I lay there in silence, waiting for a solution to become clear. With a light tap on the door, the nurse came in with one solution. I took the sleeping pill and the pain pill, turned off the light, and let the darkness overtake me.

Sometime in the middle of the night, I found myself sitting bolt upright. The hospital was deathly quiet. The white light of the moon fell on the furniture, highlighting harsh angles, turning the steel and chrome to ice. My body was wracked with sobbing that had begun while I was still sleeping. I felt wretchedly alone.

The switchboard was closed, so I couldn't call outside. Who could I telephone anyway? Why make anyone else miserable? My heart felt like it was breaking from the force of my sobs. I tore at the bedclothes trying to get some sort of control of myself. I wanted to ask the nurse if I could hold my baby for a few minutes. But, I felt too undeserving. I had awakened wanting to die. If there had been a bottle of pills right there on the nightstand, I probably would have taken them. I prayed for relief. Finally I fell back to sleep.

Two nurses came bustling in about seven in the morning. I was to gather my things and move down the hall, just off the maternity floor. The maternity rooms were full of new mothers. I guessed I wasn't considered a genuine new mother. I made them swear they would still bring my baby to me.

The new room was brighter, the window larger and the walls a brighter white. White linoleum tiles covered the floor. I chose the bed against the wall, instead of the one by the window. The corner felt more secure. The room was emptier than my other one, as it was a good bit bigger.

After settling in and cleaning up, I lay back against the pillow. This room had a radio that worked, and I hung it over the top edge of my bed so it could rest near my left ear.

Then I heard the nurse bringing my son. She was a cute nurse, delighted to tell me he was awake. I felt such relief. The night before, I had feared that I would never get to look into my son's eyes. I had wondered if the nurses fed him before bringing him to me, in order to deliberately put him to sleep. I reached out and brought him close. The warmth from his body seemed to radiate so powerfully, it flooded my whole body. As the nurse was leaving, I asked her if she could pick him up last. She said she understood.

I looked down into his eyes, and a smile welled up from the deepest part of me as our souls connected. I was amazed that a baby, less than two days old, could have such powerful eyes. He seemed so wise and sweet. I kept smiling at him in wonderment. He seemed to be listening to the music coming from the speaker on my pillow. Was that possible? I pulled the speaker down closer to his little head, so he could hear better. He *was* listening. He looked at me so intently, like he wanted to say something. After all the time we had played with each other while he was inside me, I felt that we were simply continuing our companionship. I began to talk to him. I told him all about Chris and myself and my family, and how very much we loved him. I told him everything I could think of. I strained my ears for the sound of bassinets retrieving babies. But there was a great quiet. I had to seize the opportunity. I placed my son in front of me on the bed and slowly unwrapped his blue flannel blanket. At first, I felt like a little kid about to get caught unwrapping a Christmas present before Christmas. Then my fear accelerated. Would they come in and strike me for doing this? Was this a criminal act?

The open blanket had released the heady fragrance of a newborn. Quickly I etched in my memory every inch of him. I counted, then recounted his fingers and toes, and marveled at how small, yet perfect he was. A great pride at having produced such perfection welled up in me. He was a miracle.

He had a cleft in his chin, like mine—a mark from my father's side of our family. I wondered, if my father saw he had our chin, would he be able to let him go to strangers? I let my son's fingers hold tight to mine. Then, I heard the bassinets start up.

Furtively I began to wrap him back up and realized that I didn't have a clue about how to swaddle him. Everything I did looked disastrous. I decided not to mention it, hoping they wouldn't either. The cute nurse, who had brought him to me, came back to get him. I thanked her for giving me so much extra time. I didn't want to give him back while he was still awake. I didn't want someone else either holding him until he fell asleep or putting him in the bassinet to cry himself to sleep.

I asked the nurse how he was in the nursery. She said he was very good. He never cried, except for one spell that lasted about an hour in the middle of the night—last night. She had seen it noted on his chart. I noted it, too, in amazement. I wondered which one of us started crying first. Probably, it was me. I would have to maintain a grip on myself, for his sake.

. . .

In the silence of the room, I sat very still. A new facet of myself had begun to reveal itself to me. It felt like a kind of wisdom that had always been there, which I had not acknowledged before. I began to pay attention.

I had begun to feel connected to this source of knowledge within, as my baby grew at Seton House. But I didn't know what to do with it. And I still didn't. The feeling had grown even stronger since my son's birth. It was a sense that I knew something more than most people, but I didn't know what it was that I knew.

I went to take a shower, trying to change my thoughts. As I watched the water splash on my belly, I felt as deflated and dejected as a popped balloon. I began to think about the adoptive parents. They must know he has been born, that they would be getting a boy. I didn't want to think about them, but I didn't seem able to stop. Would Sister Dominic have called them with their wonderful news? She hadn't called me.

In my imagination, I saw the beautiful, immaculate, nursery waiting for him. It had lots of toys and an antique wooden cradle. Had they selected a name for him? Or, would they wait until they saw him? Would they ask what I had named him?

I saw *her* as simply a more together version of myself, the kind of person my parents hoped I would be. Where I had failed, so far, she would triumph.

A tune played over and over in the back of my mind, a song I had played over and over again when I was little. Dumbo's mother sang it to her baby before they took Dumbo away from her, because she had lost her temper, defending him. I would play that song on my little RCA 45 record player and cry, then play it again and cry some more. The song stayed with me now, though I tried to put it out of my mind.

. . .

The bassinets began rolling down the hall again as they had, every four hours, for years.

The same nurse brought my son to me. My baby was awake again. She gave him his bottle of sugar water, and he drank it eagerly. It was a thrill to give him nourishment.

With a brisk knock, Dr. Jordan pushed the door open, walked over the end of my bed and lifted my chart from the steel railing. Reading from the chart, he said I was doing so well, I would be released by late afternoon or early evening. He glanced up at me from the chart and seemed to react sharply to something he saw. As he continued to write, he turned away from the bed, toward the window. When he was about to leave, he looked at me again.

I looked straight back at him, and with sarcasm that stunned even me, I exclaimed, "What a beautiful sight! Madonna and child."

Instantly, I shriveled in embarrassment at the revelation of my bitterness, so unused was I to exposing what I felt. He glanced at me, unable to respond, and quietly left the room. I was mortified at my lack of good manners.

Mrs. Hogan phoned. She would escort me back to Seton House that evening. I looked down at my son, realizing we had only two more visits together. How would I be able to handle this? Where would my strength come from? I held him close to my heart and tried not to get upset, for his sake. Then, the nurse came in to take him from me.

As I packed up my things, I tried to compose my goodbye to him. There was so much I wanted him to remember. I wanted to be able to imprint the truth about how much I loved him—and would always love him—indelibly on his heart. I had to find the right words, so he would carry this truth with him all of his life.

The choice of words took on an awesome weight, as I tried to compose them. I decided to say goodbye the next time they brought him, in case something happened, and it actually was the last time.

When the wheels started up for the late afternoon feeding I frantically searched the room, unconsciously seeking for some solace. I received my son in somber silence. He was sound asleep. Obviously, he was aware he was about to hear his first lecture. His eyelids fluttered, and I knew he was almost there. I held him to my heart and thought I would begin talking with him. But it didn't seem the right position. After several adjustments, I ended up cradling him in both arms, holding him in front of me. Then, I could talk to him directly.

It was difficult to sense if I had his attention. This was, after all, a one-way conversation. He was not being asked his thoughts on the situation. He was at the mercy of everyone. He could not say whether he would prefer an already established and prospering home, or one that his own mother and father struggled, against heavy odds, to create.

Deep down I was not convinced he would be better off without us, despite what everyone else believed. Yet I tried to tell him he would be going to a far better home than I could give him. My words sounded hollow. I said how thrilled his new parents would be with him, and that they would be the luckiest people in the world to have him. Nothing was coming out sounding as I had wanted. From the look he was giving me, I had the strange sensation that he wasn't buying it either.

I gave up on my speech, and pulled him close. Tears welled up, and I simply said what sprang from my heart. I told him I would always love him, that there would not be a day in my life that I would not think of him, and that he could always believe in my love for him no matter how far apart from each other we were. I told him I knew Chris would feel the same. I promised that I would find him some day, to never fear that I wouldn't. Nothing and no one would stop me from finding him when he was grown. I would live for the day when I would see him again.

The nurse came in. I gave my baby back to her. She said Mrs. Hogan was coming early in the evening. I asked her to please bring my baby one more time.

The sun was gone, so I closed the blinds, and sat wearily back on my bed. The milk welled up in my breasts and started leaking. Had my baby just longed for me, too? I rang the nurse to bring more pads to catch the milk.

I dressed in slow motion. My street clothes felt peculiar. I had not worn regular clothes in four and a half months. How long ago had I packed this dress to wear home from the hospital? I tried to slip back into the girl I had been when I had last worn this dress. But I felt the clothes were trapping me in a lie, disguising me as the person I was no longer. I wanted to tear them off and go screaming down to the nursery, grab my baby and disappear. But then I would indeed confirm I was unfit for my baby. And somehow I was terrified that, if I didn't act perfectly, they wouldn't give my son to the best family. My son's welfare hinged on my best behavior.

The nurse carried my baby son this time, instead of bringing him in the bassinet. She gently laid him in my arms. I couldn't thank her, but I knew she understood.

I held him and felt his warmth and flooded him with my

love. We sat there, not moving, suspended. I kissed him on his forehead, on his nose, and his tiny sweet lips. The nurse came to get him. I uncurled his tiny fingers from around my finger. They didn't want to let go. She lifted him from me and I watched them leave the room.

Mrs. Hogan came finally, poking her head through the door, seeming to be slightly rushed. The cold of the snowy night lingered on her coat.

I told her I had had a beautiful son. Would she like to take a peek at him through the nursery window? She said she was in a terrible rush. My docile body glanced down the hall toward the happy families at the nursery window. At that moment, some great part of me split off and went to be with him. As I abandoned my baby, my soul abandoned me, to be with him.

Chapter Six

The lights were out when I returned to Seton House. The darkness hid the sadness incubating within, sadness that seemed magnified by my absence for a few days, days spent in the brightness of light. Two approaching shadows took form. I realized the celebrity status we conferred on the newly returned mother as Anne-Marie and Nora approached. We were heroines, returning from the depths, bringing reassurance that the others would survive. I noticed a few more forms dotted expectantly down the hall, hoping to learn a little from my experience. I wanted to accommodate their need to understand what they were about to go through. Unfortunately, there were no words to describe where I had been, and where they were heading. So I pleaded great fatigue, and excused myself to go to bed with promises of full details in the morning. I understood their hunger and my obligation. I closed my door and let them go back down to the TV room and their soon-to-be exploded innocence.

Absorbed by the night, I lowered my head slowly to the pillow. Not one of the sisters had come to me. I guessed my baby was still at the hospital. I had not asked about the details of his care. Nor was I told. I didn't know how I had managed to walk out of that hospital without him. I was in a state of shock, acting "normal" but absolutely detached from myself.

From the midst of my despair I formed a prayer, woven from the last thread I had left connecting me to any kind of spirituality. The only reason I had not severed that thread was a slim hope of remaining connected to my son. I had to believe in this thread. I prayed to Mary, the Great Mother, to grant my wish:

Divine Mother, please watch over my son for me. Please love him and take care of him for me. Make sure his parents love him and take care of him the way I wish I could. Bless them and any brothers or sisters he might have. Please help him to believe in my love and feel it in his heart. And, please give him a big hug and kiss for me right now.

And then as I waited, I sensed he was being hugged and kissed by the great and sweet Mother Mary. I felt as I formed this prayer that I had invoked a profound truth, an ancient mystery. I felt the prayer settle into my heart and reach out to comfort my child, wherever he was. I had to believe in this prayer's efficacy to be able to live. When I finally fell asleep, it was like falling down into pitch blackness.

I had two full days to practice functioning with just half of myself, before my parents came. It was the same sort of adjustment an amputee must make to his phantom leg. I disconnected my feelings and was left with half a soul.

I skipped breakfast, pretending to sleep, and began to pack, putting off as long as possible the girls' questions. I could describe what happened to me physically, but I could hardly comprehend what had happened to me emotionally, let alone try to prepare them.

I searched out Nora and found her in her room. A friend was coming to get her at any moment. She still seemed flushed with the joy of her daughter. She talked as if she still had her baby in her arms. I hinted at my pain to see if I'd get a response and be able to talk with her about what I was feeling. But she was lost in a fantasy, and I didn't want to burst her protective bubble. I joined the others in the TV room. As I attempted to tell my story, I hardly recognized my voice.

No one seemed the same to me as I had thought them, before going to the hospital. Had I really spent three full months here with them, including Thanksgiving and Christmas? They were more strangers now to me than when we'd first met. As I walled off my pain, I isolated myself from feeling anything about anything. The instinct for self-preservation did not discriminate.

I was not counseled. I was not comforted. There was no mention of my son. Attention was focused on my physical well-being in preparation for my departure. There was some concern over my going back to school within a week, but I knew I could do it.

Thursday afternoon, I was given my last physical by Sister Beatrice. I was given pads to place over my nipples to catch the leaking milk. The pads had an absorbent gauze on one side and a plastic backing on the other. They left a square outline under my clothes and made a noise when I moved. How was I going to keep up my charade when I was back at school with crackling, square breasts?

Stubbly hair had begun to grow back where I had been shaved before delivery. It itched like hell. I felt exposed and self-conscious, unprotected, unnatural. How could I go back to sharing a bathroom in the dorm, breasts leaking and looking like a plucked chicken. There was also a ritual I had to perform for the next three weeks. Each time I went to the bathroom, I had to flush myself with a solution of witch hazel and warm water from a plastic bottle. How was I going to sneak around carrying that and still fool everyone that I had just returned from four months of fun in Florida?   I felt the cold metal of the examining table through my thin gown. Boldly, I asked Sister Beatrice how my son was doing. Was anyone with him? I heard her tell me he was being well taken care of. But in the pit of my stomach, I knew he was all alone. Sister did not seem comfortable having to answer my questions. Her message was that Seton House had fulfilled its part of the deal. They had taken care of me, when I had nowhere else to turn. Now I was to keep my end of the bargain by giving them my son. A primeval bargain.

I finished up the rest of my packing, then reached deep into the back of the dresser drawer and pulled out the stack of Chris's letters I had kept. I took one of my Christmas present ribbons and tied it around the stack. Someday I hoped to give them to my son. Perhaps the letters would give him some insight into what we were like. He would know that we had loved him, and how difficult our situation had seemed to us. I stuck them inside the pocket of my smock, wrapped in a handkerchief, so my parents wouldn't discover them. They did not know that Chris and I were still in touch. It was difficult to contemplate going back to lying in order to be together. How odd to be going back to being treated as a child after becoming a mother.

As I contemplated resuming my old life, I could barely imagine it. I had changed too much.

Something fell to the floor. It was an ornament from the tree. I tossed it in my suitcase, a little memento of the one Christmas my son and I had shared. Sister Agatha had given me a holy card. I tucked it into a secret place behind the cover of my missal. It was a prayer for "the baby I couldn't keep." It seemed that all I was doing was hiding the evidence of the woman I had become.

As the locks on the white Samsonite suitcase clicked shut, I heard a light tap on the door. It was Sister Beatrice. Sister Dominic had arrived. She was in a terrible hurry and needed to see me about the papers right away. It was almost six, just before dinner, my last in this place.

I opened the door to the office she was using. She stood, tall and imposing behind the desk. She remained standing while she gestured to me to take the chair in front of her. As she leaned over the desk towards me, the folds of her black veil got hung up on the back of her chair. A little space was created between the stiff white mantel that framed her face and the black veil that fell from her forehead down her back. I could see the ends of her short cropped hair, the outer edge of her ear, and part of the back of her neck. I felt like a Peeping Tom, but I was fascinated. There was something poignantly human about this little part of her that was hidden from the world, and from herself probably. It seemed so vital in contrast to her dry, gray-complected face, poking from her black habit. Paintings of the saints portrayed faces radiating a mystical rapture. Not this woman.

Sister settled down into her chair and still she seemed to loom over me. The folds of her veil fell back into place. I tried to make eye contact. She would have none of it. Instead, she fussed with the clasps of her briefcase, opened the case, and produced some papers that she laid down heavily on the desk between us. She still did not look me in the eye but leaned forward toward me. I retreated deep into the back of my chair, my shoulders hunched forward.

She looked at her watch to remind me her time was limited. In a matter-of-fact voice she told me about each piece of paper.

On the first form I had to swear I was the mother of my son. I then had to declare that I had been unmarried at the time the said child was conceived, at all times during the gestation, and at the time of the birth of the said child, and that, to the best of my knowledge and belief, the child had not been legitimated, by acknowledgment or otherwise, prior to the giving of consent by me to the adoption of the child. The next form was a "Request for Separation from Mother." It sounded more like one my son should sign. She explained that they needed this to release him from the hospital and into foster care for thirty days.

This was the first mention of a foster home. I had always been led to believe that my baby would go straight to the perfect adoptive parents. I told her under no circumstances would I sign papers putting him in a foster home. I would not sign another paper if he had to go to a foster home.

She said they did that to make sure there were no "problems." I was shocked. It made me sick to think that they could deliver only a perfect baby to their clients. What if he wasn't? Would they tell me? I suddenly had horrible visions of my baby languishing in an institution, alone for the rest of his life. And I would never know. My body began to react violently. I felt I might throw up all over her briefcase.

I told her I would sign but only on the condition that the adoptive parents would take him home within three days. Without answering me directly, she assured me I had nothing to worry about. She said it would be crushing to the adoptive parents if I were now to change my mind.

The third form she placed in front of me was a "Parent Release, Surrender and Consent to Adoption." I had to swear first that I was of sound mind and in full possession of my mental faculties. Reading this, I had to pause. I wasn't so sure. I read the rest, declaring that there had been no coercion by the agency, and that the agency now had full say over who my baby's parents would be. In other words, they owned him. In the future, I was not to interfere with my child's life in any way.

As I signed, Sister involuntarily let go of the breath we both, startlingly, realized she had been holding for the last few minutes. As she gathered together the papers, she advised me this was God's will. In thirty days they would become final.

Now, if I found a way to keep my baby, I would not only hurt and embarrass my parents, be a blight on society, doom my child, ruin all Chris's chances and mine for a decent life, I would also be defying the will of God.

I watched, mesmerized, as the briefcase closed, the clasps snapped and locked. Sister grabbed its handle and lifted it up off the desk. I watched it fall down by her side. It seemed vaguely incongruous to see a nun with a briefcase. Her long wooden rosary beads clunked for a minute, till each found its proper relation to the other. The doorway framed her as she turned to me and said, "May God have mercy on you."

I was unable to stand up. She left me there in the office and disappeared into the cold January night with the most profound and fateful papers I would ever have to sign in my life. The consequences of those signatures would permeate every aspect of my life, my son's life, Chris's life, and many, many other lives, forever. I had had no legal counsel, no psychological counseling. I was nineteen and alone. I sat for a while, stunned, overcome by my desolation. Finally, I turned the lights off in the little office and left.

At dinner the others seemed subdued. I didn't know how to say goodbye. I would never know how things turned out for any of them. Another veil dropped over me to dull the pain. As each veil of mourning dropped, I grew less and less aware of what was happening inside me. Each deadened the pain at the core of my being, my longing. I began to feel like a casual observer of my own life. But I could still function, even if my goodbyes came out sounding hollow to my ears.

I said goodbye to Sister Bartholomew. I didn't go to the TV room to be with the others. Instead, I showered and went to bed. I lay down on my back, remembering the nights I was so full of my baby. I said my prayer to Mary, praying that she would hold him for me as he lay alone in the hospital nursery. Then I sat straight up. Had Sister Dominic taken him away with her? I had no idea what her plans were. She hadn't told me. It made sense that she had taken him with her. Otherwise she would have to drive back to Richmond again in a couple of days. But perhaps the adoptive parents were from Virginia? I panicked as I realized I had no idea *where* he was.

———

There was a light knock on the door. Sister Agatha poked her head in to say that my parents had arrived. She had been talking with them. They were so happy to have me back. Then Sister took the Christmas box, and I took the rest and followed her rustling skirt down the long darkened hall for the last time.

My parents stood before me in the foyer. They were so happy to see me and amazed at how wonderful I looked. That was the closest they came to acknowledging all that had happened. Perhaps they were advised that the less said the better. I'm sure they were quite relieved that there were no visible signs of my recent pregnancy. The pretending could start right away.

They hugged me. Dad went out to load the car. Mom was lovely with Sister, and Sister was just as charming and bright back.

I stood quietly apart from them and looked at the spot where I had always imagined the adoptive parents would be standing when they saw my baby for the first time. I had imagined their delighted expressions. I hoped that wherever it happened, the sun would be pouring down on them, and that it would be a sacred moment for them. I felt faint.

Dad came back in and said everything was all set. I shook Sister Jerome and Sister Beatrice's hands goodbye and thanked them. They stood at the door and waved as we climbed into the car.

As Dad was about to turn on the ignition, I asked him to wait for a minute. There was something I wanted him to know. I had rehearsed the words in my mind, since returning to Seton House. Because we never talked about feelings, I felt I would be jumping over a horrendous chasm to make my little speech. But I had to.

"Dad," I said. "I just want you to know, that I will never, ever do anything to disappoint you again."

The words came out, choked up and clumsy. After hearing them said out loud, I wanted to take them back. I was afraid of what would happen if I uttered one more word. It took all my strength to fight back my stinging tears and keep from screaming. I didn't know why I needed to be so stoic. Perhaps, I felt that if my suffering wasn't obvious to them, from the very nature of my experience, that they would never truly understand anyway. I certainly wasn't the first young mother discharged without her baby from a home for unwed mothers. If there were any doubts, my parents needed only to look back at the waving, smiling sisters, so enthusiastically blessing our decision, as we drove away down the drive.

I sensed that my father was quite moved by my statement. It left him speechless. It had never been easy for him to express his feelings, but I had never seemed to need him to, since I could see them in his eyes. Mom half-turned, resting her arm along the back of the front seat, her fingers nearly touching my father's shoulder. Her face was turned almost, but not quite, far enough to look at me.

"We don't ever have to mention this again," she said. "Soon, we will all forget that it ever happened."

But I would have to bring it up one more time, to see how they felt about my marrying Chris now. I wanted to wait until we got home, and I could sound out Mom first. I knew that if I mentioned Chris's name right now, my father would either run up the back of the car in front of him, or put me out on the curb.

Mom began to chat, filling me in on all that had happened in my absence, trying to cheer me up. Again, the great Civil War heroes of Monument Avenue loomed majestically overhead. Furtively, I peeked through the spaces between them, hoping to catch sight of Richmond Memorial Hospital.

The farther we drove from Seton House and Richmond

Memorial, the more surreal everything seemed. I observed, with fascination, the everyday coming and goings of people in their cars and walking along the sidewalks. They all seemed totally unreal. If I were to reach out to touch them, they'd disappear into the ether. How was I going to fit back into the real world?

I stared intensely into the face of each person who crossed the street in front of our car. Would you really mind if I kept my baby, and married his father, even though it would be after his birth? Would your children really taunt him in the park and call him "bastard" the rest of his life? I wasn't certain.

I felt dreamier and dreamier the farther away we drove through the rolling hills and beautiful countryside. I closed my eyes to it and tried to sleep and find some place in my mind to go where there wasn't any pain. I could not stop the tears that kept stinging the corners of my eyes.

Finally, we drove down Friendly Road, the main artery to the suburbs in my hometown. We pulled off Friendly Road and turned onto our street. As I looked at the neighbors' houses, I wondered if they realized the incredible power they held. Our worrying about what "they" thought was such a huge reason for my baby not being in my arms as we drove up our driveway. And we barely knew most of them.

As the engine was turned off, my parents seemed to let go of all their worries with a huge sigh of relief. The ordeal was finally over. They had *their* firstborn home again.

I felt like a stranger walking into the house. Dad went back to the office. I excused myself to go clean up and lie down. I know my mother wanted to do something for me, but short of finding a way for me to keep my baby, there was nothing she could do.

After going through my witch hazel purging ritual in the

bathroom, I went into the bedroom I shared with Janice. She was still at school. I propped up several pillows, so I could sit up and try to think clearly. My old bedroom, in which I should have felt so safe with myself, seemed to have turned on me. Its familiarity was in stark contrast to how unfamiliar to my old self I had become. I knew there was nothing in this world that I would have to live through that could be worse than what I had just experienced. Since I'd survived this, I could survive anything. Still, it was with a terrified heart that I tried to compose my request for permission to marry Chris now.

I got up out of bed and smoothed my clothes. They were hanging on me. I had never been so thin. I took a deep breath to compose myself, turned the brass knob to my bedroom door, and summoned up hope one last time.

I found Mom in the kitchen, fussing over soup, preparing a tray for me. She said it was so good to have me home again. She asked me to come out back so she could take a picture. I had to find a jacket, as it was cold. I scooped up our toy poodle, Gigi, and walked out into the damp afternoon air. It was a jolt after the stuffiness of the house. I held Gigi in my arms, barely aware of my need to hold something to make the picture complete. Mom fiddled with the camera; I waited patiently. She snapped two pictures. I scrutinized her intently, waiting for the perfect moment. Had she noticed I wasn't her little girl anymore? Did she realize I never could be again—didn't want to be?

We came back inside and took our soup into the family room. I sat down on the sofa, and Mom sat in the wing chair to my right. I had a surprising sense of being her equal now. But we hadn't evolved to this point together, so it felt disconcerting. I didn't know how to be diplomatic, so I went to the heart of my speech.

"Mom," I said. "Chris and I have continued to write and talk.

We are still in love." She didn't fall apart over that, so I continued. "He came to the hospital the night after our baby was born. He got to see him through the nursery window but they wouldn't let him see his face." I paused, waiting for some reaction beyond pleasant attention to my story. Maybe she tried to stay composed in order to help me. I didn't know. There was a gulf between us; I couldn't seem to cross it. Perhaps it was impossible for anyone to understand if she hadn't experienced it as well. Maybe what I was trying to say sounded like a foreign language to her. But she herself had had four children, one only four-and-a-half years ago. I wanted her to hold me in her arms and comfort me after all I had been through alone. But I wasn't going to beg for her consolation. Several of the girls at Seton House had parents who barely spoke to them, they were so enraged that their daughters had gotten "knocked up." I had to be grateful, as Sister said, for my parents' continued support of me. I said in a weak voice, "Chris wants to get married, and I do, too."

There was a pause. "Well," Mom said, "you know your father and I would help you in any way. But, of course, you would have to move away to another state, at least for a while. Otherwise, your father would stand to lose his job. What would people think? How could we explain everything otherwise?"

I tried to picture myself alone with a new baby and a new husband in a strange state, with no friends and no family around. I tried to imagine Chris agreeing to make such a sacrifice for me. I did not think of myself as worthy enough to ask such a thing. I would be asking Chris and our son to live in shame with me, for probably the rest of our lives, from what I could foretell at that moment. When would we be allowed out of hiding, out of exile?

I said that I couldn't imagine doing that. And she said, "Fine. We will never bring up the subject again."

With composure, I placed my soup bowl back on the tray and pulled myself up from the sofa. In a flat voice, I excused myself to go rest, since I had to leave for school in two days. My breasts filled. Milk leaked all down my shirt. Was my baby needing me? Was he crying? Was someone picking him up, comforting him? I lay down on my bed, eyes staring blankly up at the ceiling. I felt almost catatonic.

Muffled noises came to me. First, the front door slammed and Janice arrived home from school. There was a quick, furtive warning, in a stage whisper, not to go into our room. I was home from school with a terrible case of the flu. The phone rang in the kitchen. Then, I heard Janice scurrying down the hall to grab Ellen, just before she turned the handle of the bedroom door. Gigi barked after them in all the excitement. In a louder voice, Mom said, "Keep her away. Carol needs her rest to get over the flu."

One lie fed on another. When would the necessity for them end? Would the priest count these "necessary" lies as sins? Did my mother even have the nerve to confess to them?

On Sunday morning, Mom and Dad and Janice and Ellen went to Mass without me. I lied and said I couldn't go, because I felt I needed to conserve my strength for the ride back to school. Actually, I had no desire at all to step foot in a church. It would have been too ridiculously hypocritical.

In the emptiness of the house, I thought about my son being one week old. Memories of that Sunday, a week ago, were so fresh, it seemed I had stepped right back into them, and it was happening all over again. It was now one week closer to the time I could start to search for him.

Chapter Seven

My ride back to Winthrop College arrived. The four in the car already were upperclasswomen whom I knew, but not well. They were all aware that I had skipped the last semester. So I had to answer their curious questions about my wonderful semester sabbatical in Florida. They probably knew the truth but out of kindness and politeness let me continue the charade. It was an unwritten understanding that, whenever a girl disappeared for a while, she had been pregnant.

My breasts leaked, and I furtively double-checked to see if the gauze pads had caught the evidence of my lie. They had, this time.

I remained quiet most of the way, as the others were close friends and filled up the time with their banter. I could stare out through the rain-blotched window and dream about my baby. I would be able to call Chris tonight.

When we pulled up to the dorm, I thanked them for the ride and hauled my heavy suitcase up to the room. I was not supposed to lift anything yet. But I hoped it would not cause any internal damage.

Blair was sitting on her bed, along with Barbara and Sheila, our suite-mates. They were waiting for the cafeteria to open for dinner, and jumped up to greet me. I sensed that they held a part of themselves back, not knowing what to expect from me, after what I had been through. As they watched me, they were observing, as well, what they feared most for themselves. They thought I had been unlucky. But I could not think of my baby as bad luck. He was too beautiful.

I had been hoping that I would be absorbed immediately back into my old life the minute I walked into the room. It didn't happen. Everything seemed one-dimensional, unreal. I seemed to be listening to my voice from the corner of the room, up on the ceiling, by the window. I knew that it was no good. I couldn't relate to my friends anymore. I knew something that they didn't know. I had had a baby grow inside me, experienced labor, given birth. I had held my own flesh and blood in my arms. My whole body was longing for him and my life could no longer be like theirs, or like mine had been.

My breasts swelled and ached and dripped milk. I tried to cover the mess by holding my purse up to my chest. The gauze crackled. Hoping to appear casual, I walked over to the dresser, keeping my back to them. I think my friends were a bit frightened of me. Indeed, I frightened myself. They asked me if I wanted to eat with them. I declined, saying I needed to unpack, and asked them to bring something back. I just wanted to be alone.

Late that night, when I couldn't sleep, I wrote Chris. I had tried to call him, to tell him it was impossible to get married. But I could not gather enough courage to tell him directly. I was too heartsick and ashamed.

As the days passed, I fought hard to become my happy-go-lucky self again. Perhaps—after my breasts dried up; and my hair, where they had shaved me, grew back in; and I no longer had to purge myself with witch hazel; and the memory of the weight of the straps used to tie me down during labor faded — I could be like my old self. Then, perhaps, I could shake this unspeakable sadness and stop fearing for my sanity. But I became more and more immobilized. I would find myself sitting in a stupor on my bed after classes, hardly able to move a muscle against the weight of the oppressive air surrounding me. When I attempted to communicate, words seemed to get caught up in the thickening web surrounding me, and hung there. I went through all the motions of living, not caring about anything, feeling utterly isolated and alone. Not one person had prepared me for these feelings and I assumed they were unique to me, caused by my own lack of character.

I knew the very last day that my son would still be truly mine and Chris's would be Valentine's Day, thirty days after I had signed Sister's release papers. My mind lethargically took note of each day that passed, as Valentine's Day approached. All the while, I was picturing my son as promised: happy and smiling up at his perfect and beautiful new mother. His successful father had probably bought him tons of toys. They introduced him to all their friends as their son. There was probably not even the faintest trace of me left in his memory. The sisters had assured us of that. His parents probably assumed they had a "tabula rasa." After seeing his soul in his eyes, I knew they didn't. I wondered if they ever thought of me. I didn't have a sense that they did.

It was hell not knowing where they lived. I imagined them everywhere. I felt safe as long as I stayed on campus, and didn't have to see mothers and their babies, and wonder if each one was my son.

———

I always stayed up until everyone else was asleep, so they wouldn't hear me crying. The only way I could get to sleep was to let myself cry first. There seemed no other way, short of stashing a fifth of vodka under my mattress. The night before Valentine's Day, I prayed extra fervently to Mother Mary, begging her to help my son understand, help him to know how much I loved him and would always love him, help him to have a happy life. I prayed in panic.

On Valentine's morning I awoke nauseous, ran to the bathroom and threw up violently. I thought I had the flu. All day I felt wildly disoriented.

Sister Dominic did not call to force me to come face to face with the reality of that day. In the quiet of her office, twenty-five miles away, she took out the papers I had signed barely four days after my son's birth, and countersigned with her own name, sealing our fate.

———

Since Winthrop was a women's college, it was as deserted as a ghost town on the weekends, as desolate as a place could be. Even a student without personal problems would end up in despair by Sunday night from sheer boredom and loneliness.

In an effort to get me out of my depression, Blair and some

other friends urged me to start dating again. They were all having fun dating guys at a nearby Catholic men's college. I knew I couldn't go on like this forever, so one weekend I joined them. They fixed me up with a date whose father had a ranch with horses. We went riding for hours. My horseback ride awakened a fine madness in me. I saw the beauty of nature again, smelled the richness of the soil and leaves and pine. I felt laughter bubbling up. Except now the beauty touched me too deeply and reopened my wound. I wondered if I ever would escape from my sorrow.

My date had a cache of bourbon, and we all started drinking late in the afternoon. As the alcohol seeped into my bloodstream, my body, for the first time in almost a year, had relief from the weight of excruciating sorrow. The relief was pure bliss. The contrast took me by surprise.

After dinner, my friends went off to be alone with their boyfriends, and I was alone with my date. I wished I were a magician and could turn him into Chris.

No one had told me that the plan was to spend the night at the ranch. My date and I, deserted, stared at each other in discomfort. I poured another bourbon and wondered what he would think if he knew the real truth about me.

There was a huge fire going in the big stone fireplace of the cabin. The heat didn't reach the couch where I was sitting, so I bundled up in my winter jacket. I stared at the bright embers as my date went out to get more wood. What in the world were we going to talk about? How could I talk about myself, without mentioning that I had a two-month-old son, that I was trying to get over having to give him up, and that I was now sure I would never fully recover? How would I ever be able to get to know someone as a friend again, without revealing the most important part of who I was? But I knew I had to learn how to lighten up, or I would be sitting alone in the dorm every weekend. I needed to escape, forget, not wallow around in my depression.

My date returned. His voice droned on, telling me about himself. At Seton House, we had debated often about when would be the best time to tell a man we were interested in that we had had a baby. Some said only when there had been some sort of commitment. Some said never. Since we were "damaged goods," we thought we would have to be grateful to find a man so kind as to care about us, despite our "horrible mistake." We would have to grovel in our gratitude. We would be indebted to any man who not only forgave us for not being virgins, but overlooked the fact that his first child would be our second. We obsessed about our broken hymens, and were completely un-witting of our broken hearts, broken spirits, broken minds.

I silently watched my date stoke the fire with the great wrought-iron poker. He went outside and returned with three more logs, and threw all three on the fire. I was amazed at myself for sitting in silence for so long. Light banter used to come easy to me. Now it was hard.

My date was older, twenty-three. He was here for only a brief visit, so he was safe. Actually, the perfect man with whom to test the waters. In the light of the now roaring fire and my several bourbons, as he turned back towards me, I knew that he was going to try to kiss me.

I pulled my jacket closer, despite the fact that the heat had now reached the couch. As he put his arm around my shoulder, I said there was something he needed to know about me. To my astonishment, the words came out sounding like I was apolo-gizing for leading him on, and warning him he had been kind to a social leper. I was putting myself down before he had a chance to.

As I told my story out loud to this stranger, I sounded like a stranger to myself, confessing deep self-hatred. Instead of communicating the beauty of becoming a mother, I spoke of my shame. I wasn't sure where that came from. I thought I had salvaged my pride. Now I saw, as I spoke out loud to this man, how untrue to myself I had been.

He listened attentively and probably would have been kinder if I had been kinder to myself. I became acutely aware of his shift in feelings toward me, from amorous to brotherly. That suited me fine.

In the sober light of morning, I felt embarrassed at my revelations of the night before. I wished I had not felt forced to speak the truth before I was ready. My date didn't mention it. I was quite glad he would be leaving town.

It was dark in the Winthrop College post office, and silent for once. I worked the combination on the tiny dial of my P.O. box and flipped open the little door. There was a single letter from Chris. As I pulled his letter out of the box, I felt his presence. I could feel the sorrow in his letter, without reading it. I closed the little door softly and stood in the dark. We found we needed each other even more now. We weren't supposed to still feel regret. The pain was supposed to have dissipated by now, but it was getting worse for us. At least we could help each other with our profound guilt and the anger we felt for having listened to all the wrong people and not ourselves. We could not speak the unspeakable even to one another, that we had given our own baby to total strangers and abandoned him to an unknown destiny.

I knew the time was coming when I would lose Chris, too. Being with each other would remind us too much of our loss.

We had no choice now but to go on with our lives somehow. But we needed each other too much to let go just yet. No one else was there for us as we grieved. No one seemed to want to be.

I didn't go home again for two months, and I only went then to see Chris and my friends. I kept putting off going back, as it meant I would have to tell more lies to my parents, lies that I wasn't seeing Chris, lies that I had forgotten everything, lies about who I was, bold-faced lies that I was happy. The strain of maintaining the façade was too great. I avoided home as much as possible. I avoided talking to them. I knew they were hurt, and maybe even bewildered. However, I had no resources left in me with which to deal with their hurts even though I felt guilty for causing them such misery.

Walking out the door for my first secret rendezvous with Chris since our baby's birth, I sensed my dad's anger toward him. It almost terrified me enough not to risk getting caught. But we *had* to see each other.

I didn't know my emotions were still so completely raw until I saw him. I felt shattered, yet more alive. Seeing him, I had feelings again. At the same time, I knew I couldn't live with them. I would have to go dead again in order to live.

As I drove past Charlotte on the way back to college, I began to shake. I thought it was from the memory of hiding out there at Tessa's. But could it mean that my son was close by? Sister Dominic had told us that the children would be placed far from their mothers. If I knew he were close by, I would have wandered the streets, looking in every baby carriage. I would probably have dropped out of school to find him. My worst nightmare was that someday I would look into his face and not know he was my son. I got cold and clammy at that thought.

Back at school I spent endless hours daydreaming about what my son was like, what his parents were like, where he lived. I vacillated between believing he was greatly loved and fearing he was all alone. Often, as I wandered in my thoughts under the ancient oak trees lining the campus, I wondered at the normality of the lives of all the people I walked past. Sometimes, under the oaks, I thought I heard a baby crying.

We were studying Greek plays in my drama class. I had loved the drama course I took my freshman year, yet this class, like my others, had ceased to hold my attention. But something the professor said cut through my fog. It must have registered first at a deeper level, as my eyes were already wide with horror, before I turned from the window to stare at my professor. Dumbstruck, I tuned into the story of Oedipus unknowingly marrying his mother and killing his father. I could not stop giggling. Life seemed suddenly a sick joke. In a perverse way, this was the first bit of instruction I could relate to since coming back to school.

My professor shot me a look of surprise. The bell rang and the class was dismissed. Stepping out of the century-old building, I felt the rain splash on my hands as I tried to protect my books from getting soaked. I lifted my face up and felt rain and tears.

As Easter vacation arrived, I began to get excited. This would be my first holiday celebrated at home in a year, since my banishment. I wondered about the other girls from Seton House, and if they were faring better than I.

Jessica would serve as the go-between for Chris and me. After arriving home Good Friday afternoon, it took six furtive conversations to organize our meeting, and another to cancel it after Mom insisted I go to the stations of the cross to set a good example for Janice and Ellen.

Cool air from some infinite source within the cold stone pillars of the church rushed up into my face to greet me as we entered. It mingled with the incense. The old wood floor creaked as we shuffled into the pews and the kneeler landed with a thud, announcing our slightly late arrival. I could still feel the holy water on my forehead.

I had not set foot inside a church since Seton House. I did not even try to listen to the priest's words. Their cadence served only as a background to my own thoughts as I recalled the previous Good Friday. I quickly wiped away the remaining dampness of the holy water from my forehead, and smoothed back my hair in order to get a grip on myself and get back to reality.

A baby cried in the back of the church, and shortly afterward the great doors slammed as the mother rushed out with her infant, so as to not disturb the service. I tasted tears on my tongue and didn't have a Kleenex, or a prayer of stopping them. I looked toward my mother. Her face was filled with devotion, as she and the others prayed along with the priest.

At station of the cross number thirteen, Jesus falls the third time. Blurred, my eyes tried to follow the priests' procession and refocus on the flames of the tall candles carried by the altar boys. It was dark. Only a couple of candles lit the altar. Purple velvet shrouded the statues. The air was thick and the incense made it even heavier. Everything was dying that night. I seemed to be breathing the acrid dust kicked up by the movement of the procession through Calvary. My mouth could taste the grit and sweat in the leaden air.

Outside, a storm was approaching. After the service, the first drops of rain greeted us. Mom, Bob, Janice, Ellen, and I piled into the car and rode home without saying a word to each other. It felt like we were unrelated. Something was happening to our family. I watched the headlights of our Chevy Impala. Perhaps it would be impossible for us to be a happy family with such an important member missing and unacknowledged. We filed out of the car and into the house, sullen as we had been all evening.

In church on Easter Sunday morning, everyone seemed to look startlingly "new," and not comfortable with themselves in all their finery. When I was young, I had a funny walk, peculiar to Easter Sundays. In order to keep the bottoms of my new patent leather shoes from scuffing, so that they would still slide smoothly over the living room carpet when church was over, I walked on the edges, or minced my steps. It never worked. Despite my efforts they were scuffed by the time we returned home. Now I wondered what my son's first Easter outfit looked like. I took the holy card, hidden in my missal, the card given me by Sister Agatha, and read it over three times, as an incantation to make his first Easter a happy one.

After the service, my parents went off to play golf. That afternoon, Chris climbed out of his family's car, came around, and held my door open for me. Nervous about his visit, we had parked on the street in front of my house rather than in the driveway, even though we thought we could count on one safe hour before my parents returned from their golf game. Janice had always had an enormous crush on Chris. She'd begged me to bring him by.

As we walked up the slight incline of the driveway, Janice came out the front door and cut across the lawn to meet us halfway. She was delighted to see Chris. We walked halfway up to the house and stood in the protective shade of the poplars that separated our home from the neighbors'. I felt breathless and exhausted, as if I had climbed up a steep mountain. I stood on the hot asphalt driveway, absorbing all the heat it was releasing, just as I had steadily absorbed the rage my father felt toward Chris. Chris was the scapegoat, the lightning rod for everyone's anger. I needed to let him go on to something better than that, just as I needed to let my baby go to a better life. Or so I told myself.

Back at school, very late that night, the pay phone rang. The hall counselor came into the room and said it was for me.

It was my father. He'd found out somehow and he was livid that I had seen Chris and that he had even come to our house. Janice was grounded for allowing it, and he threatened to call Chris the next day. I pleaded with him not to call him or his parents. I was mortified at the idea. I promised him, if he wouldn't call, I would finally end the relationship.

I walked back down the dormitory hall to my room. Blair was still up. She was a great listener, and I sat on the edge of her bed and tried to sort out my choices.

I went to bed undecided.

———

Running like an undercurrent through my days was a growing anxiety about my son's welfare. Sometimes I had a dreadful sense that something was wrong with him. And then, as if to compensate, I had a fantasy that I played over and over in my mind, many times a day, every day, that his placement had not worked out. That Sister Dominic would call and ask if we wanted another chance to keep our baby. I could not imagine the adoptive parents as dead in a plane crash or car accident, so how to dispose of them in the right way was a problem. I finally worked it out. I had her get pregnant and not be able to manage two babies at once. That way, everybody would be happy.

—————

Chris's birthday fell on the coming Sunday, Mother's Day. I came home from school for the weekend as did Blair, my roommate, who lived nearby. Chris and I arranged to meet secretly Saturday night. I had told him of my father's threat, so we both felt terrified of being discovered as we settled the rendezvous. Jessica was away at school, so Blair helped.

Blair's home was beginning to provide for me the warmth I no longer got from my own family but so desperately needed. Her family's kitchen was big and welcoming, and always a bit lived-in looking. Blair's mother was easy company. Their huge old Dalmatian shared a cup of coffee with her every morning. She didn't ask a lot of questions.

Saturday night, as planned, I went to Blair's, to play bridge. Chris was going to come by, as soon as he could after dark. Blair's mother had a passion for bridge, and the trick was to get her to understand that at some point during the evening, I would have to stop playing and talk with a friend outside. I had to go out as soon as I heard the car in the driveway, no matter where we were in the bridge hand. We didn't want her to know I was seeing Chris; we didn't want her to be in a position of having to lie for us.

It was an enormous effort to concentrate. Providence provided. I was dummy when I saw Chris's headlights flood through the living room curtains. The tires crunched over the gravel and then stopped.

I walked to the dark corner of the driveway and let myself into the front seat. It struck me that he looked a bit disheveled. I had never seen him anything but beautifully dressed. No longer allowed in my home or in the homes of any of my friends, he must have begun to feel like a common criminal. I tried hard to hold myself together. But when I looked at him, pain flowed through me.

The air was cool, yet still warm enough that we did not need sweaters. The crickets chirped. A fragrant jasmine breeze floated through both open windows. I was aware of the brightness of the stars, and how the moon lit up the huge magnolia blossoms.

Chris, with frightening gravity, said he felt something was really wrong with our son. Terror ripped right through me as I heard him voice out loud the awful premonitions I had been having. He wondered if we should call Sister Dominic.

I didn't believe she would tell us anything. I was afraid to talk to her. A great heavy silence fell over us. I stared straight ahead at the magnolias. Their huge blossoms turned into the bright oncoming headlights. I gasped. The silence closed back in again.

I heard my voice say, "We can't see each other anymore." I felt his body take the blow, then he sighed. "I can't handle this sneaking around to see each other anymore. I can find no more strength to fight my father's wishes. I can't persuade him to change his attitude. I don't see any hope for us. Remember that I will always love you."

I couldn't stay one more second in the car. It hurt far too much. I tried not to watch as he pulled out from the driveway. But I turned just in time to see his car lights disappear.

It was Mother's Day, but my son was with another mother. I prayed my prayer to the Great Mother Mary to hug and kiss and watch over my baby. When I did my dream prayer, I always made sure it was early morning or late at night, when my baby would be sleeping, and I would not interfere with his waking life. As I said my prayer, I let myself feel so near that it was as if I went to him myself and lifted him out of his crib, and held his body close and told him how much I loved him. And then I felt extraordinary peace. I smelled the sweetness of his little head, and it took my breath away. The moment felt like eternity.

In church on Mother's Day I wondered about his new parents. Did she think of me? Had she wiped me from her mind, as Sister Dominic had undoubtedly advised? Or was she having a difficult time erasing me and wondering why she couldn't, perhaps believing that not forgetting was a deficiency on her part? She had more right to my son than I did; she was married and had money. Did my bitter thoughts prove how unworthy I was? I glanced across the sea of summer hats and white gloves, lace veils bobby-pinned to sprayed and lacquered bouffant hairdos framing self-righteous, holier-than-thou Sunday-morning looks. Was it a sin to keep thinking of my son as "my son"?

Chapter Eight

I rarely ever cried again, except when alone. I was proud of my lack of tears. It showed strength of character. I wasn't a weak, sniveling woman. I threw myself into school life. Dated. Took exams.

I finally had the opportunity to see Florida for real. I stayed with my suite-mate, Sheila, for a little vacation, right after school. She fixed me up with an old friend who was wonderful and seemed to care about me a great deal. But it was too difficult. The night before I was to go home, I broke down completely and told him the truth about myself. I told him not to call me after I left. I felt he deserved better than me. I couldn't let anyone really love me again.

I went back home to take summer school classes, so that I would graduate on time, as if I hadn't missed that semester. I was obsessed with graduating on schedule.

I worked again at J.C. Penney's, played a lot of bridge, went out with old friends, and filled every waking moment with something to do, something to read, someone to talk with. If I was still for even a minute, a cold panic would grip me.

On my way back to begin my junior year, I was surprised to be shaking again as we drove through Charlotte. My apprehension actually seemed greater, not less. My breath became shallow, and the old panic began to well up. Then, as we approached Winthrop, I calmed down. What was it? Was Charlotte haunted? Was I?

Required classes were finished and I could start on my major. Despite the specter of training a real, live mouse in experimental psychology, and having to take statistics, I had decided to major in psychology. I did not want to be like the others who were going for their teaching certificates, only to marry right after graduation and begin having kids. I didn't want to do merely what was "expected" of women. I felt too different for an average life. Having lived in many areas of the country other than the South, and therefore being more sophisticated than my Bible Belt counterparts, I thought this logical. I didn't think to attribute my rebelliousness to having already had a child, and being irreparably and permanently different anyway. It certainly never occurred to me that I might simply feel angry enough to need to do the opposite of what I was supposed to.

The experimental psychology classroom was spacious. Dr. Murdy came up with a little mouse in a cage and placed it on my desk. My heart was beating wildly with trepidation. It took me all of two seconds to fall for my mouse.

The professors in our psychology department were behaviorists. Dr. Murdy seemed to believe that B.F. Skinner was just short of a god. As he explained operant conditioning and Skinner boxes, he stood leaning against the blackboard, tie loosely knotted, tweed jacket draped loosely. His pipe was always tilted up to the sky. As I listened to Dr. Murdy's lecture, I watched my little mouse run around in his cage. I decided to name him Herman. He looked like a Herman, and I hoped a name with a studious ring to it would inspire him to greater feats of accomplishment in the Skinner box. My academic future rested on his ability to learn quickly. We were to conduct a series of experiments, designed to illustrate the power of positive reinforcement. Today's experiment would be the foundation for the rest, which would grow more and more complex. Each Monday, our mice had to perform an increasingly difficult task. It was not uncommon for students to spend nights and weekends in the lab with their mice, trying desperately to get them to learn their role.

I carried Herman over to the Skinner box by the window. Before I put him in it, we had an intense conversation on the importance of learning quickly. I thought him attentive. Sure enough, he was pushing the lever in no time, the first to be trained. He was so bright that I was always the first out of the lab. I felt we were partners and I often stopped by just to say hello.

Herman's brilliance confirmed me as a psychology major. I was fascinated with everything I was learning, yet my Catholic conscience kept me anxious. Many Catholics believed that the study of psychology was opposed to religion. A great many of the Southern Baptist students felt that psychology majors were on the road to hell. It was seen as narcissistic mumbo jumbo designed to weaken character, not strengthen it. If you were a psych major, it was assumed you were crazy yourself. In my case, I felt they had a point as I studied for my course in abnormal psychology, searching for a way to understand what had happened to me.

Our class visited the South Carolina State Mental Hospital on a field trip. After the public relations tour through the shining new buildings housing the rehabilitative patients, our professor asked to see the belly of the place. Our guide was reluctant, her eyes frantically searching for a superior to rescue her. No one was around. Despite her misgivings, she led us out down a path splitting the lawn, until we reached a dusty courtyard. The buildings surrounding the barren square seemed ancient. Patients hung out the windows and put on a "loony" show for us, so we wouldn't be disappointed with our visit.

Our professor asked our guide to be sure to take us to the worst ward. With a look of "you asked for it," she unlocked the first of a series of doors. As each door opened, the din of raving voices grew louder. We were in the women's ward that housed the severely schizophrenic and catatonic. Everything seemed the color of dust. It was as if a storm had left a film over everyone and everything, a kind of pinkish-beige hue.

There were some twenty-five women in the ward. Many rocked monotonously, either standing in one spot or sitting on the floor or on a bed. Others lay curled up in fetal positions. Not one looked at us. One woman kept sweeping the same spot on the floor with a worn-out bristle broom. It was pitiful in there and filthy smelling. What had made these women end up here?

Our guide asked that we not look into the padded cell and disturb the patient. Well, of course I immediately dropped back from the group to peek through the small window in the locked door. It seemed imperative that I look.

She was wrapped in a straitjacket, lying on her side as if she had been flung there. Her sandy blonde hair was matted and fell over her face. Her long, slender legs were tucked up under her chest. She looked to be my age. Her face, the chiseled line of her cheeks and jaw, bespoke a lost beauty, though her wide-open blue eyes were sheer emptiness. Mine filled with tears. I wanted to go into the cell and talk with her, help her. I asked a million questions about her as we were whisked off the ward.

In preparation for our next field trip (to the South Carolina Home for Exceptional Children, "exceptional" being perhaps one of the original euphemisms), we studied the work of Harry F. Harlow. Harlow's experiments compared monkeys raised with surrogate "mothers" made of bare wire to those raised with surrogate wire mothers wrapped in terry cloth. His experiments concluded that the baby monkeys preferred the warmth and comforting texture of the terry cloth mothers even over the wire mother who provided a bottle. The intensity of response to the surrogate mother was directly related to the interval of delay after birth before the surrogate mother was introduced. Those with the surrogate mother from birth bonded far more strongly; the bonds weakened in proportion to the delay. In adulthood none of the monkeys raised with either type of surrogate functioned effectively. Only those raised with their own mothers became healthy, mature monkeys. Studying the material was horrible for me.

I stared, riveted by the photograph in my textbook of the frightened little monkey, clinging desperately to its cloth "mother."

Over and over again I read one passage from Harlow's essay entitled "The Nature of Love":

Although the fact that mortality and morbidity rates for children separated from their mothers are higher than those for children who are not maternally deprived, what essential factors the mother provides is unknown. Certainly, there must be factors other than food, clothing and warmth, since these are provided for infants in institutions.

According to extensive research by Dr. John Bowlby, "The mental health of children is tragically damaged by separation from their mothers." The severity of the damage depended, of course, on the quality of the substitute mothering experience, and the length of delay in providing an adequate substitute, and the number of such substitutes during the first three years of life. To some degree, the separation created a "characteristic impression" on the personality. The children appeared emotionally withdrawn and isolated. They failed to develop loving ties with other children or with adults. There could be found a "sociability in the superficial sense, but if scrutinized, it would be found that there are no feelings, no roots in those relationships." A "lack of emotional response, a shallowness of feeling, and little or no evidence of any real attachments having been made" characterized their social interactions. Was this fate preferable, I wondered, to living with a mother who had sex before she was married?

Too bad Harlow didn't think to observe the mother monkeys after their babies were taken from them to be raised by cloth-wrapped, wire surrogates. Did they just kill the mothers, since they had no more use for them? Too bad. They missed their chance to do a study to see if they became psychotic, or catatonic, or schizophrenic, or suicidal, or alcoholic without their babies. They should have observed them to see if they could live normal lives and forget.

Or, if they lived, did they, too, become depressed, distant? Would they form healthy relationships? Would they fear making love from the terror of becoming pregnant again? Would they be able to nurture their future offspring as effectively as "normal" mothers? Or would they, perhaps, become infertile?

If they had studied the mothers, maybe I would have known what to expect for myself. Did they feel isolated, as I did now, feeling all this pain, having all these questions? And what about the fathers? What about Chris?

What was happening to my baby?

The facility housing South Carolina's "exceptional" children was brand-new. But not one tree or flower bed broke the flat monotony of manicured lawn that led to the building. The air was oppressively humid, the sky a heavy gunmetal gray.

In contrast to my anticipation before visiting the state mental hospital, I dreaded coming to this place. I had tried to get out of it, but couldn't come up with a convincing excuse. I couldn't explain that my profound reluctance sprang from a terror of possibly seeing my own worst nightmare come to life: *My son would be there.*

Whenever the fear of not knowing where he was, or how he was doing, leaped out of control, I ended up imagining him lying alone in a crib in an institution like this one. No one would tell me, and he would waste away to nothingness without my knowing.

He had seemed perfect in every way, but in class I had read that hydrocephalus developed three days after birth. I panicked. Hydrocephalus, water on the brain, enlarged the head to three to four times normal size and caused retardation. I had not been with him long enough to know, and Sister Dominic had implied that only perfect babies were adoptable. What happened to the others?

By the time we walked up the interminable concrete walkway and reached the entrance, I was petrified. We were greeted by the administrator. Without much preamble, she swung open the doors to the first ward, the one for the most profoundly retarded. There were perhaps twenty cribs in this one small room, yet it was eerily silent. From unfathomable depths of nothingness, eyes stared at us, the childish faces all wrong.

The administrator pointed out each child, explaining different etiologies and ages—six years, twelve years—as a gardener would describe particular types of flowers and shrubs. The face of a pansy could yield more spirit than these children's faces. According to the administrator, most parents never came back to see their children. It was too painful, and the children wouldn't know them anyway.

"In the corner," she said, "is Jonathan, who is profoundly hydrocephalic."

My body pivoted around immediately to face my worst fear. In stunning contrast to the other nineteen children lying in their cots, Jonathan was sitting up, defiant of the weight of his heavy head. Such an enormous head to have grown from so frail a body! Such courage. He observed us with what I felt was intelligence. There was a knowing in him, a spark in his eyes. All the while, the administrator was describing his vegetable-like state. Hadn't anyone looked in his eyes, or felt his presence? I wanted to touch his shoulder, take some of the burden from him. I had an urge to communicate something to him. I didn't know what. But we were instructed not to touch any of them. It might set them off. She said Jonathan was sixteen, an unheard of lifespan for a hydrocephalic. What did he want to live for? What did he know about life that I didn't know, that kept him wanting to live? What fed Jonathan's will?

Deep in the Smoky Mountains, there was a traffic jam. A great tree lay beside the road, felled by the winter winds, roots upturned, exposed and vulnerable. Without its powerful roots, the great tree had no dignity. All that had been majestic about it had vanished.

My brother Bob and I were on our way to a new home in Akron, Ohio. My father had been transferred, and my family had moved right after I began the semester. Bob was a student at Clemson University, a couple of hours away from Winthrop College, so we were traveling together to our new home. We had not seen it at Thanksgiving; the trip would have taken too long. I had spent last Christmas in a strange place about to surrender my baby. This Christmas, I was going to a strange community, exiled from the hometown I had loved. Perhaps it would be a chance for me to start fresh. I wondered if my parents thought so.

We drove up to a pretty, two-story colonial, surrounded by woods. The lights of the Christmas tree, sparkling through the bay window, greeted us first. The colored lights danced on a soft dusting of snow. It could have been a greeting card. What had happened to Mary and Susan and Anne-Marie and Nora and the others, I wondered. Were they having a hard time, too? I missed them, though I only knew their first names.

This was my baby's first Christmas. He must be crawling now. Was he standing? Trying to walk? What were they planning to give him for Christmas?

The warm air of the house, full of the aroma of baking cookies, wafted out into the cold night air. Mom and Dad, Janice and Ellen ran to greet us. But my memories seemed more real than what I was experiencing. It was almost as if I could walk through the next door and be there all over again. I would have walked through in a second, too, just to be pregnant and have my baby with me again, to feel whole again.

This year we did more things together as a family, since Bob and I didn't know anyone in Akron. Ironically, every loving thing Mom tried to do made the holiday worse.

Tim, a fellow I had started dating, was coming up to visit after Christmas. Tim had graduated from a small selective men's college in North Carolina. Now he was in graduate school at the University of Kentucky. His father was a minister. I doubted he would approve of his son dating an unwed mother, if he knew. I had told Tim about my son, and he had sworn never, ever to tell anyone else about him. With Tim I began a long-distance romance. Given the separation, I was able to avoid any real intimacy and yet have an ongoing relationship. The past semester, I had gone to many Sigma Chi parties with his fraternity brothers, dating them as friends. They knew Tim was my beau. I enjoyed their company a great deal, and I kept myself safe this way.

The more I tried to push away thoughts of not being with my baby and to stifle my memories of Seton House, the more they met me everywhere. On Christmas Eve, in the middle of last-minute shopping, I found myself, as if I had just awakened, standing in front of a department store display of a manger scene. Salvation Army bells clanged close by and snow flurries spun around the heads of bustling shoppers. I stared at the empty crêche and wept.

I pulled myself away from the window and walked on. Taunting images rushed up at me. A little baby. Is this his first Christmas? A big teddy bear, an old wooden rocking horse. Could that be my baby with that tall blonde woman and her handsome husband? Could they, by some fluke, have moved to Akron, Ohio, too? I stumbled home.

Yes, Mom. My shopping went great. Yes, the stores were crowded. Everything was wonderful. Couldn't have had a nicer time. I wanted to keep to myself, but the strain began to get to me. I counted the days until I could return to school.

That night we had eggnog together and turned all our attention toward Ellen. She was only five and still believed in Santa Claus. She recited "'Twas the Night Before Christmas" to us and we made a big fuss. We set out cookies for Santa.

Did my baby like the Christmas lights? Were they magical to him? What was waiting for him under the tree? God, how I wanted him with me. Christmas would never be the same to me without him. I should be holding him, pointing out the ornaments. I wanted to read "The Night Before Christmas" to him, as I remembered my parents reading it to me and bragging about how I had memorized it at a young age. Again, unbidden, came the flashbacks to our little tree at Seton House. Amidst all the anguish of that Christmas at Seton House, I had been happier by far than I was this Christmas.

My baby's first birthday was on a Monday, the first day after winter break. I was probably fortunate to have a full day of classes to distract me.

Afterward I decided to walk over to the church. I pulled open the huge slate gray door and let myself in. One older woman was lighting a votive candle. Her black veil fell down to her shoulders. She seemed to be in mourning. My veil was back at the dorm, so following established protocol—and feeling dumb about doing it—I pinned a piece of Kleenex to the top of my head. Women, but not men, had to cover their heads. Why?

Heavy incense hung in the air and enveloped me as I knelt down in the pew. The only light came from the stained glass windows.

I waited for my memories. Nothing came. I tried to retrieve one tiny detail—any fragment—but my mind was stubbornly blank. I tried a prayer. Nothing. Everything in the church began to annoy me. A man in his fifties, sallow, blockish, dressed in a wool suit that matched his sandy hair, walked in through the side door and knelt heavily in a pew. The woman in mourning, black hair streaked with gray, olive complected, recited her rosary, kneeling before the votive candles. They both mumbled their prayers out loud, disturbing the silence I sought.

All I could think about was missing dinner at the cafeteria. Maybe I had been lying to myself this whole year, *making* myself believe I was missing my baby and feeling such overwhelming love for him. Maybe my pain and my tears were simply to assuage my guilt, purge my sin. I could remember nothing, I could feel nothing.

The man in the wool suit hoisted himself clumsily out of the pew. The loud bang of the kneeler reverberated through the church as he pushed it back up. The woman by the votive candles was startled momentarily.

The light no longer streamed through the windows. The sun had finally set. The color was drained from the stained glass.

I slid back onto the pew. My knees were sore. I looked around at the different stations of the cross hanging on the walls. Their depictions of the passion and suffering of Jesus left me unmoved, bored. I was not only seeing what a sham I was, but becoming sacrilegious on top of it. There was not a thing I cared about. That day a year ago could have happened to someone else. Had I imagined it? Did I have a son?

I gave up, gathered my books together, rose and sidestepped out of the pew. Did Chris remember it was our son's birthday? I asked myself. Then, as if I had been hit by a tidal wave, I fell back, fell to my knees and wept and wept. I went through my whole package of Kleenex and then pulled the one off the top of my head and used that. I wept until I had no tears left.

I said a prayer for my baby, and I sat back, spent. Yet I felt filled with new life. I wondered what time it was. I could see that it was dark outside. I wanted something to eat, and to get back to my room so I could be near my clock at 9:51 P.M.

I left the church. Memories came flooding at me as I crossed the campus. My breath kept catching as I took in each image with a twinge.

Back at the dorm I sat cross-legged on my bed, books propped on my lap and scattered all around me. I watched the clock. At 9:51 I wished my baby "Happy First Birthday." No matter how he celebrated with his family all the rest of the day, that moment, I felt, would always be just ours.

Chapter Nine

YE SHALL KNOW THE TRUTH
AND THE TRUTH SHALL MAKE YOU FREE

I stopped, drawn to the words etched in the shrine of concrete on the old brick wall of the Humanities Building. I
wondered why I had not paid attention to them before. The
words were not new to me.

I released myself from their hold and rounded the building
to the entrance, and then walked down the hall to the most
exhilarating class I had yet taken. I sat down in the front row,
next to my new roommate, Anita, and looked up into the kindly
face of my philosophy professor, Nolan P. Jacobson. Behind
Anita and me sat twenty-five women born to and raised by
dyed-in-the-wool Southern Baptists. As Dr. Jacobson began to
speak about his belief that, in the near future, there would be a
great blending of Eastern and Western religions, the girls
behind us squirmed, waiting for the wrath of God to descend.
When Dr. Jacobson announced that one of the subjects we

would cover was reincarnation, I was thrilled. The subject had fascinated me since I debated the idea in tenth grade.

My other classes included human development, marriage and family, and the dreaded statistics. I sat through those classes wrapped up in wonder and pain simultaneously. We studied pregnancy, fetal development, birth, infant and child development. I sat silently in class with my secret. I was hungry for every bit of information that would give me a clue to my son's life, that would help me follow his development.

I waged a private battle with those who espoused the theory that environment had a greater impact on a person's life than heredity. I was hoping for at least a fifty-fifty split between heredity and environment, so that I could feel that my life would have some impact on my child's. Blind panic welled up at the thought that, when we met, I would be a total stranger to him and of no more significance than a passerby on the street. There had to be an inheritance from me, and from Chris, that would keep us connected.

I wondered if his new parents believed that they could write their own script for my son. They would be wrong. I had looked deep into my son's eyes. There was already a sense of a strong individual. He had a personality of his own. None of the texts addressed that telling look. I knew it was real. I knew what every mother knows—that a child's innate individuality was there at birth, and even before. I had not held a bundle of white cotton fluff in my arms, nor was I made of terry cloth and wire.

It was Easter. I was visiting Tim's home in Kentucky for the first time. The tap on the guest bedroom door was light but insistent. I sat up, trying to appear respectable as Tim's mother let herself in.

Without really looking at me, this formidable woman set down a little tray bearing a demitasse of strong espresso, and left the room. Her plump face was a mask of politeness, but she closed the door too quickly. I inched toward the corner of the bed, avoiding the cloud of disdain she'd left behind.

I understood where it had come from. Tim had admitted telling his mother that I'd had a baby. In his mother's eyes, Tim was perfect, as was his younger sister, who was a year ahead of me in school. The night before, I had listened to a litany of her accomplishments, including the fact that she had recently been nominated to *Who's Who in American Universities and Colleges*. The only time Tim's mother ever looked me in the eye was when she was bragging about her children's accomplishments. I sensed a clear message that I was not good enough for her son. If I could have, I would have packed my things and left their house. I had never felt like a coward, but I was a coward now. I was furious with him for telling her.

I let my hand play on the heavy wood bannister as I walked down the staircase. Tim was at the bottom, waiting to take me to his father's church. This would be the first Protestant service I had ever attended. I studied Tim all the way to church. Why hadn't I seen what a mama's boy he was?

"He maketh me to lie down in green pastures. He leadeth me beside the still waters. . . ." The sermon was thought-provoking, not preachy. No statues stared back at me, loaded with the energy of millions of projections. It felt clean and simple in their church. And they certainly sang better than Catholics.

Back at Tim's, his mother served a traditional Southern Sunday brunch: fried chicken and biscuits, creamed green beans, homemade pies. It was delicious. But I couldn't feel comfortable in her presence. Then I left for the long drive back to school, alone.

Great trees hung over the centuries-old stone walls built by the Kentucky slaves. The walls lined the road for miles, protecting the bluegrass pastures and the grazing thoroughbreds. I wondered if maybe I had been too sensitive about his mother. I vowed I would show *everyone* that I was not damaged, that I was still a decent human being.

It was a nice thought and, back at school, I buried myself in classes and Sigma Chi parties. It worked pretty well, until I read in the chapter, "Deviant Sexual Behavior," in my abnormal psychology textbook:

> Other types of psychopathology, such as manic reactions, may also be of etiological significance in promiscuous sexual behavior. There is a failure to either develop normal inner controls, or a lowering of these controls as a consequence of severe emotional maladjustment. In a study of 54 unwed mothers ranging in age from 15 to 39, Cattell (1954) found psychopathology in every case: 30 had character disorders, 17 were schizophrenic, and 7 were neurotic.

Had the researcher assumed that, since they were unwed mothers, too much sex had caused the women's psychological problems? Too much sex didn't cause 100 percent of married women to suffer psychopathological disorders, did it? Had he looked more closely, he might have found the psychopathology of unwed mothers sprang from not being with their babies.

Most of the girls at Seton House had been with their boyfriends only a few times, and if more, it was because they had been in a long-term relationship. Not one had been promiscuous.

Pondering this remarkable research, I felt a little less crazy, knowing that I really *was* crazy, as I had occasionally suspected. At the same time, I felt a little more crazy, knowing *how* crazy I was. One hundred percent in any study is a phenomenal statistic. Perhaps Tim's mother had been right.

After the semester ended, I went back up to Akron for the summer, to work, but I missed my old hometown. Akron was not it. By the end of August, when Bob and I were on the road south again for my senior year, I was in a heavy depression. The car seemed to be moving through molasses all the way there.

Sitting in our room, Anita and I plotted ways that would help us get through what seemed to us an interminable year. I didn't know why I needed to be in such a hurry, as I had no plans for after graduation. We decided to involve ourselves in campus politics and run for office. I ran for school vice president and came in second, then I ran for campus coordinator and won. Anita edited the literary magazine, and we were both in the student government. I had a heavy course load, taking one extra class to make up for the semester lost. Soon, I was taking diet pills (which were really speed) to stay awake so I could do all this. But in reality, I needed them to fight off the horrible anxiety and depression. I seemed fine, hopped up on the diet pills, busy with classes and student life, but even after a few solitary minutes I would feel panicky. My temper was short; Anita stayed away from me. So did everyone else. I began to feel abandoned, even though I was the one alienating everyone. So I took more diet pills and felt I was some sort of genius when I was high on them. Then, I got sick with a horrible cough that kept everyone awake. As they tried to help me, they began to confess how concerned they had become about my temper, and how it was affecting everyone. The next day I went to the infirmary, too sick to go home for Thanksgiving.

For two days, I slept. The campus was eerily silent and empty. I was the only patient for the Thanksgiving weekend.

I floated in and out of strange dreams and I was grateful that the Darvon kept me mostly unconscious. Something had gone very wrong for my son, I felt, and I wanted badly to talk about this premonition with Chris. But I thought I must be simply delirious; I couldn't trust my feelings anymore.

Classes had resumed for two days by the time I was finally released from the infirmary. I couldn't remember ever being so sick before. I was still weak, but more depressed than anything else. I had to get busy and divert my thoughts. Longing for my child did me no good at all. I came out of the infirmary as if out of a long dream.

Some things were clear. I would not take any more diet pills. I would apologize to everyone, especially Anita, and I would turn over a new leaf. I began to pull myself together, but my shaky self-esteem had definitely taken a severe blow. I never wanted to seem any way different from the others. It was like walking around with a constant fear my underwear was showing. I had secrets to keep, and it was hard work.

———

I was taking four classes dealing with children. Fieldwork began for my preschool education class. It required many hours observing at the on-campus nursery school, a cute little red brick building.

My son was almost two. As I watched the children, I tried to imagine what he was like. Was he blond and active, like the little boy building tunnels and bridges with wooden blocks? Or was he quiet, like the one by the easel, absorbed in the primary colors? Or the shy one, observing everyone else? He couldn't possibly be like the mischievous kid, throwing sand at all the other children in the sandbox. It was so hard not to know.

I made dean's list for the first time in my life, and dated Tim over Christmas in Akron. We hadn't seen each other during the semester. Just after the new year, Bob and I headed back down to school for my last semester.

There was a message waiting for me from one of the Sigma Chis. I had thought they had forgotten all about me. They wondered if I could possibly come the next night to act as hostess at a pledge function. They would send someone to get me, since I didn't have a car, and would drive me back that night before the dorm closed at eleven. That would involve four hours of driving for someone. I was really flattered that they wanted me there. My battered self-esteem began to repair itself a bit.

When I walked into the Sigma Chi house, I was greeted so warmly that the dregs of my depression melted away. As I spoke with old friends and met the new pledges, I kept noticing one of the brothers whom I had never gotten to know. He was very tall and blond with an enormous smile. He walked up to me with his big grin and thanked me for coming. His name was Jerry. He had organized the party and said the others had insisted that I be there. Now, he knew why. I wanted so much to be able to accept and enjoy the compliment from Jerry, yet in the back of my mind I knew tomorrow would be my secret son's second birthday. Was he talking yet? Who did he look like? Was he happy? Healthy? Alive? If only I could know that, perhaps this panicky feeling I lived with all the time would lift. My feelings this birthday were different from the last, the pain dull now, the memories muted. Back at Winthrop, I commemorated our moment again, at 9:51, and said a longer version of the prayer I still said for him every night.

———

Jerry called. He wanted to come down to Winthrop to see me, and did I have a friend for his roommate Frank. I asked Anita, and she said "Great!" When Anita and I greeted them in the parlor, Jerry's grin was infectious. When I looked up into his eyes, I felt I was greeting an old friend. It felt so comfortable.

The evening air was warm, like late spring, although it was early February. We went to the Holiday Inn for a beer. Bars in South Carolina served beer, and mixers for the hard liquor customers, who would bring their own in a paper bag. We sat down at the dimly lit bar. Scattered throughout the room were traveling salesmen at round black tables, all in various stages of inebriation. South Carolina had a law that forbade driving with an opened bottle of liquor in the car. Therefore, people would sit around in bars until they finished off their fifths, so no alcohol would be wasted.

Anita and Frank were absorbed in conversation with each other, as Jerry and I were. We talked on and on, and we laughed a lot.

Deep into the evening, Jerry turned toward me, his face serious and concerned. I was puzzled at his sudden shift of mood. Then he said he had a question to ask me, and before he did, he wanted to be sure that I knew that he was only trying to clear up something he had heard that couldn't possibly have been true.

My body tensed. My mind would not let me believe the worst.

Some of the fraternity brothers had told him that I had missed a semester of school because I had had a baby. It was strange, I could not remember an out-loud acknowledgment that I had had a baby, not since I had left Richmond. But then I heard the words again, as he prattled on.

I found myself outside in the parking lot, beside Frank's car, sobbing uncontrollably. Jerry ran up and caught me and held me tight. I sobbed into his shoulder, "It's true."

"Oh, my God," he said, and held me tighter. I had not been comforted so before. Jerry said, "I feel so honored that you could tell me the truth, and I'm moved by your courage."

When I finally pulled myself out of his arms, I was breathing easier. I asked Jerry how he knew. Tim, he said, had told the guys, just after we had started dating.

I felt humiliated and enormously betrayed. I doubted I could ever face any of them again, but I was so grateful to Jerry for his kindness, though I thought I would never see him again either, now that he knew the truth about me.

First thing the next morning, I marched off to the phones. I was in a white rage as I dialed Tim's apartment in Lexington. He was there, and I let him have it. How dare he betray my confidence? How had he been able to look me in the eye for the last year and a half? To tell the whole fraternity in a Sunday night session and to let me believe that no one knew. To let me be humiliated like that! I never wanted to see him again. I hung up. So much for Tim.

Jerry and I continued to see each other. I began to care about him. My feelings for him became deeper, but then I grew too frightened to commit myself. So I kept things light between us.

Classes were stimulating, and my professors seemed to be

taking an interest in my work. And Anita and I were on a roll in the student government. In April, eight of us flew to Mobile, Alabama, for a conference of leaders from the southeastern schools. It was a real honor to be chosen to go to this conference. If they knew the truth about me, they'd probably banish me, I thought. It was a constant struggle between belief in self and my intense shame. I lived my life despite myself, and if my feelings became too severe, I would drink to blot them out for a while.

I glanced up over the top edge of the student newspaper, just long enough to locate Anita and the others already seated at a table in the cafeteria. They waved to indicate their location, and I resumed reading, as I walked down the center aisle to the food line. The lead article concerned the selection for *Who's Who in American Colleges and Universities*. I scanned the list of predictable names, and then stopped, stunned, when I saw my own. My feet would not move forward, as I reread the list to make sure. I stood rooted in the center of the aisle, so that people had to make their way around me. I swung from complete elation, to horror, to delight, to guilt, back to pride, and then to extreme embarrassment. I went straight to my friends' table. A little voice down deep whispered that I really did deserve it and I took in everyone's congratulations with a smile as I contemplated, with sweet satisfaction, the reaction of Tim's mother.

It was the fraternity's beach weekend, traditionally held on Mother's Day (when else). Most of the girls were still getting dressed. I was too impatient to sit under my hair dryer to ensure the perfection of my flip. My creamy white Levi's were stiff as a board from heavy starch. They were perfect.

I found Jerry, standing on top of a sand dune, presiding over the grill. I felt drawn to him for a moment, then again became frightened. He watched me walk toward him, a smile on his face but a serious, sad look in his eyes. For me it was one of those eternal moments. The spell broke. I handed him a glass of Scotch and got busy with the food preparations. I tried my best to forget that it was Mother's Day weekend and also the weekend of Chris's birthday. I always associated the two. The effort made me melancholy. Then, it was late, and we were both exhausted from the week and the long drive. Jerry and I walked down to the beach. He wanted to explain how the sleeping arrangements were set up. This was the first time the issue of sleeping together had come up. To this point, I had stayed in the dorms with the other dates. We were both embarrassed.

I wanted to sleep some place alone with Jerry, and not share a room, even though we would not be doing anything more than just that—sleeping. Jerry could have easily arranged it, but he refused. When I got upset, his face in the moonlight became a battleground of conflicting emotions. There was a long silence between us. I could hear the waves crashing in the dark.

"There is something I haven't wanted to tell you," he said, "but now you need to know, to understand why we can't have our own room." Apparently, it was a tradition in the fraternity that, every Sunday night, the weekend was rehashed and notes compared about who "scored" and who didn't. Of course, everybody claimed to have "scored." (Tim had told everyone about my baby in one of those sessions.) Everybody had expected Jerry to make love to me, since I, of course, was no longer virginal. Jerry wanted to be able to say each Sunday night that he hadn't even touched me, which was true. In that way, he said, he hoped to end the rumor, to restore my "honor." He did this, he said, even though sometimes he wanted me more than anything. We had to share a room with others, he said, because he did not trust himself to be alone with me. So we did.

The next night Jerry asked me to walk down the beach with him. A couple of his close friends were paying particular attention to us. They seemed to know something I didn't. Jerry was nervous and withdrawn, and I held my breath most of the way, until we settled down into the darkness.

He began by talking about his long-term girlfriend from home, in Houston. She was asking him to make a choice. He cared for both of us, he said, but I was graduating and moving back up north, and he was from Houston. He saw little hope that we would be able to keep our relationship going. But, he said, that was not the only basis for his decision. He felt she needed him more, that our relationship was not based on reality. He believed that a relationship could not stay magical forever, that its foundation had to be everyday living. And besides, he said, I was far stronger than she was. I didn't really need him. *It wouldn't matter as much to me.*

I wanted to scream. I broke down. Jerry looked at me, helpless. He said he had no idea at all that I would have this reaction. He thought nothing upset me, that I didn't feel deeply. And he was right. Only once had he seen me show any real emotion.

I got up and left Jerry sitting in the sand, completely be-wildered, and went up to our room. I couldn't stop crying. When Jerry came up to see me, I told him to go away. I lay on the bed and wailed for hours.

By the morning, I didn't blame him. She deserved him more than I did. I felt I had no right to anything. So I dealt with this the only way I knew how to handle any loss in my life, large or small. I buried my feelings.

———

My college career was nearly over. In the middle of exam week, Anita found me studying in a quiet spot in the dorm kitchen. She told me to drop everything and hurry down to our room. I couldn't imagine what had made her so excited, since she was usually calm and poised. I walked through our doorway and the room was completely dark, except for one candle. It was filled with most of the girls from the floor. One of the girls had been given a Hindu record, and they waited for me to arrive before replaying it. Winthrop was relatively cloistered from the rest of the country. Even though it was mid-1968, and Eastern mysticism was spreading through campuses like brushfire, it had not yet reached our campus. Nor did I know what marijuana was, and I had never smelled incense, except in church. The country roiled with political protest, student revolts, and even assassinations, but we had yet to experience any of it.

I settled myself in the last space available on the floor and closed my eyes as Anita insisted. Vibrations started through my body, gently at first, as the resonant voice chanted *om*. There was no music, only that one sound, and it grew in intensity until I found myself buoyed up by it. I craved that sound. It transported me. When it ended and the lights were flipped back on, I didn't want to return to earth. But the girl who owned the record had to study. Dr. Jacobson had said that "om" was the sacred sound of the universe, "amen" a derivative.

Packing my trunk, I uncovered my old missal. I had not opened it in over a year. Hidden in the secret place was the old holy card from Seton House. Would I be leaving my baby here in the South? Would he sense I was gone? This was a horrible feeling, almost as if I were abandoning him all over again. But he could be anywhere. I rocked back and forth, to check my rising anxiety, and told myself he was with a good family.

Jerry came to my graduation, and sat with my parents. I had my education, one of the things for which I had given up my baby. It was an empty, meaningless day.

Chapter Ten

I found a job in Ohio as a social worker. At the time employees of Goodrich and Firestone were striking. It had lasted for months and benefits were running out. Proud men with frightened families were lining up for food stamps. I was assigned a caseload to release an experienced worker to help the strikers.

I wanted to work with the deprived and helpless. I wanted the harder, more desperate cases. Instead, I was given the easiest caseload, consisting of eighty families in a relatively safe district. There was so much paperwork that few hours were left for home visits. But I made one that I can never forget.

I parked under the shade of an enormous elm near the porch of an old, peeling, clapboard house. Despite obvious poverty, the little street retained a dignity rare in the slums. I walked up the cracked concrete walkway. The wooden screen door rattled when I knocked. From inside came footsteps and a small child's voice. There was a long hesitation before the door was opened. Our visits were always unannounced, to catch any cheaters off guard, and it embarrassed me to have to behave in this way.

A tall woman in her early twenties, hair short and wispy, peered at me through the screen. Her little two-year-old son held onto the edge of her brown cotton uniform. She was a single mother receiving Aid to Dependent Children. I introduced myself as her social worker. She invited me in, but said she had only a few moments. She had to get to work. As I checked on her salary and rent, I knew she was over her maximum allowance. I didn't say anything, but she did.

She begged me to consider letting her stay in her house. She couldn't bear to live in a more rundown neighborhood and expose her son to dangers. She hoped in six months to have saved enough to get off welfare completely. The father of her son had abandoned her when he learned she was pregnant and her parents had rejected her. No one was helping her.

The little boy's eyes never left his mother's face as we talked. As I watched her speak, with her son draped around her knee, I knew I could have been this woman, if I had only had the courage. She had come from a family that would have enabled her to go to college, have a career, dress well. She could have had all that, if she had given her child up for adoption, she said. Instead, she worked as a waitress at the Brown Derby, lived on the edge of the slums in a strange city, and didn't have enough money to spare to go to the movies. But the love she and her son shared for each other was beautiful and plain to see. She sat on the edge of the frayed sofa, the only piece of furniture in the room, and was a whole person. I sat at the other end, only half a person.

She had to rush off to work. I told her not to worry. I would keep her secret. We left together. I watched her walk down the sun-dappled street with her son, as I sat in my brand-new gold Mercury Cougar.

For the first time, I took full responsibility for not keeping my son. I wrapped my arms around the steering wheel and buried my head, letting the full force of my shame and sorrow wash down over me. I fought to shove down my self-loathing. I managed to turn on the ignition, put the car into gear and get myself back to the office. I was functioning. That was the bottom line.

In early fall, Dad came home with the news that he was being transferred to New York City. The move was scheduled for mid-November, just before Thanksgiving. I contemplated staying behind and living a predictable life in Akron, but the opportunity to experience New York seemed too exciting to pass up. I went, too.

Emerging from the caverns of Grand Central Station, I hailed my first cab and took it to Anita's apartment, where I would be staying until I got settled. My delight was so infectious, the cabdriver couldn't have been anything but friendly.

I could see Anita loved her new life. When she'd applied for the job as airline hostess, she had never flown in an airplane and was terrified, but she loved flying now. I had to step over bodies or mattresses to get to any part of her apartment. She lived in a crash pad for hostesses flying international routes for TWA. The five girls living in the one-bedroom apartment were in a continual state of arriving, waiting on call to depart, departing, and sleeping at odd hours. I fit right in, in a corner, temporarily.

As soon as I hit the pavements, I realized that I didn't want to go back into any form of social work. This was the Big Apple; I wanted a glamorous job. But I had little luck in my search, and I was looking at the bleak prospect of accepting a job in personnel at Blue Cross and Blue Shield. Dad had tried to pull strings to get me into an advertising agency, which was my heart's desire, but I had muffed the interview. I didn't even know what a copywriter was.

On a whim born of desperation, I tried a new employment agency. As I entered the dingy offices, I sternly lectured myself on the folly of following unrealistic dreams. This was the end of the road. Tomorrow I would accept the job at Blue Cross. As the secretary perused my application, she noted I was from Akron. We have someone from Akron working for us, she remarked, and led me into an office. The interviewer was great. She had the openness of the Akron people I had known, and the directness of New Yorkers. And she had a possible opening as a gal Friday at a small advertising agency for me.

Walking nervously through the great art deco lobby of the Chrysler Building, I found the bank of elevators that would take me up to my appointment. It didn't begin auspiciously. Could I type? No. Had I ever worked answering phones or as a Gal Friday? No. Could I write? I liked writing, my squeaky voice piped out. Did I have any artistic abilities? Not that I ever knew of.

The glow was gone from the sidewalks and great buildings of the city. The winter chill ripped right through my thin coat. I walked up Fifth Avenue, not wanting to go back to Anita's quite yet. Part of my panic was a fear that the Blue Cross job would not be challenging enough to quiet the haunting pain I still felt when I had time to think. Everything I did had to be larger than life to compensate up for giving my baby up.

But, by a miracle, I got the advertising job. I started work on Sunday, December 1, because they were shooting a television commercial that day. My initiation into the advertising world was also the actress Sandy Duncan's first time filming a television commercial. The client, Leeming Pacquin, a division of Charles Pfizer, had had a huge success with Hy Karate, the first men's cologne to be advertised heavily, and now wanted an equal success with a teenage girl's cologne named Skinny Dip. The name and the storyboards were giving the network censors a fit. In the midst of the sexual revolution, and while we were all seeing the hideousness of the Vietnam War fully revealed on the TV news, these guys were still worrying about the implications of the name Skinny Dip and panicking over Sandy Duncan's towel slipping too far from her neck.

It was exciting. My very first week, I took a limo to Peter Max's apartment to deliver proofs of a TV commercial for our product Nutrament. It was the first psychedelic television commercial. Within a month, I knew my way around, but for the most part, my job was answering phones. Dad worked in the city and would call every day and instruct me how to answer with a cheerful, upbeat voice and manner. (Thanks, Dad.)

I moved out of Anita's place into a huge apartment on Seventy-ninth and Riverside when a TWA hostess whom Anita knew needed a roommate. The apartment seemed so far away from the "action" that, after a month, Peg (my new roommate) and I moved back to the swinging East Side. We traded our big empty place on the West Side for a tiny one-bedroom penthouse apartment above a bar called The Flower Pot. The rent was so high, we had to get another roommate. The bedroom had only enough space to fit a bunk bed and a trundle bed. To get to the bunk bed, you had to climb over the trundle. But we didn't care. We had arrived. Fortunately, both our third roommate, Trela, and Peg flew for TWA International and were gone for long stretches. Rarely were we all there together.

I began to meet people and to date. But I still felt unable to connect. Sometimes, after a date I would find myself in an enormous depression. I couldn't tell them who I was—a mother. Nor could I ever be the girl of their dreams. And each time I had to lie to someone about who I was, I was further cut off. Or maybe I was afraid, equating love with loss and not wanting to be vulnerable.

New York City daily presented me with a challenge. Did I want to fight or give up? It was enlivening. If I wanted to make it from one block to the next, to cross a teeming street before a cab hit me, I had to keep up the pace. The pressures affirmed life. Would I stay safely bolted up in my apartment? Or would I see what I was made of? Because it never stopped demanding more, the city was my great teacher, forcing me to deal with the pain and sorrow and joy of living with the best and worst of human nature. Every day on my way home from work I walked by the New York Foundling Hospital and thought about volunteering, but I wasn't strong enough, yet. Whenever I passed a Catholic church, I would go in and light a candle for my son.

When I was hired, I had been promised that at the end of three months, I would be trained in one of the departments. I was made a junior copywriter. It turned out to be an extraordinary opportunity. Within a few months my line, "Makes a girl feel pretty," was used to advertise Skinny Dip cologne. It was the jingle for their TV and radio commercial. Working on the Clairol accounts, I named one of their products, Lemon-Go-Lightly, and designed the package. I loved the business.

Like graduating from college, having a successful career was an item on the list of good things that would happen for me as a result of my accepting the decision to give up my child.

One Saturday Peg and Trela were both away and I was gathering up my laundry to do a wash when the doorbell chimed. I saw through the peephole that it was Peg's blind date from a few nights before. I invited him in, moving the laundry basket out of the way so he could sit on the couch. Ron had on a leather jacket and cowboy boots, and he had longer hair than anyone I had known personally. I thought he was extremely attractive, although wild-looking, and figured he must be a hippie. He was actually a graduate student in finance at Columbia University.

As we talked he seemed pretty normal, although certainly not the arch-conservative type I was used to. He kept me company as I did my laundry. He kissed me during the spin cycle.

By the beginning of my second year in New York, Ron and I were seeing only each other. Slowly, Ron had helped me feel safe. He knew about my baby, and he listened to me. We had been raised in different faiths, but that did not matter to either of us.

Before we got married, I asked Ron to promise me two things. I felt so strongly about these two wishes that if he did not agree, I knew I could not marry him.

The first was that Ron not interfere when I eventually searched for my son and that Ron accept him, since I wanted my son to be a part of my life, if that was at all possible. He agreed.

The second condition was that we not raise our children in any formal religion. Instead, we would teach them ourselves what we individually believed and let them make the choice when they were older and knew their own minds. Again, he agreed.

We were married by both a rabbi and a Catholic priest the day after Christmas 1970 in my parents' home in Connecticut. My folks raised no objections to my marrying out of our faith. Mother knew and accepted, with sorrow, my break with the Church. She may have felt I took after Dad, who had been raised a Southern Baptist. He went to Mass every Sunday without fail, yet he had never converted. But my mom could have no peace if I didn't receive the sacrament of matrimony. A marriage outside the Church would in effect be living in sin. As long as the priest did his part, she wouldn't care what happened afterwards.

Soon after our wedding we left for San Francisco where Ron had been transferred by the New York-based brokerage firm he'd gone to work for.

Our one-bedroom apartment was right on the water in Sausalito, with huge windows that opened onto the bay. It was like living on a boat without the motion. I didn't have a job but felt sure, with my portfolio, I would find one quickly. It was a bigger adjustment than I'd foreseen, though. I was beginning my marriage far from family and friends, knowing no one. Mood swings plagued me; I would weep for no apparent reason. I began to gain weight; my fear of turning into a fat housewife was coming true. And yet, otherwise we were very happy.

When I had not had my period for four months, I went to the doctor for a pregnancy test. It was negative. A couple months later, the test was still negative. So I couldn't blame my mood swings and weight gain on that. But I could not find a job. It was more difficult to break into advertising in San Francisco than I had supposed, especially since most of my work in New York involved new product development. I despaired and spent much time alone. The empty days began to fill with memories I had hoped would remain suppressed. Pain again began to haunt me. The one thing that kept me from succumbing was my certainty that I would find my child someday.

One spring afternoon, while sunbathing, I noticed that when I lay on my stomach I could feel a lump that felt like a large tumor. I made an appointment to see my gynecologist the next afternoon. I had been charting my basal temperature for the past two months to see if we could find the cause of my missed periods. I was quite worried, anticipating the worst.

Ron hitched a ride to work and left me the car. As the time came to set out, my spirits soared, which seemed a little weird considering the circumstances. The sun poured through the roof of my car. By the time I reached the Golden Gate Bridge, I was practically euphoric. The sunshine on the bridge had an otherworldly intensity; all my senses were so acute. I barely slowed for the tollbooth and drove right through without paying. I just suddenly knew, as I crossed the bridge, what my doctor was going to tell me. Police whistles sounded and I glanced back through the rearview mirror to see three toll-takers waving at me to stop. I stopped, backed, then grinned from ear to ear as I gave them their money.

My doctor said, "My dear, what is the matter?" When I told him I had felt this lump, he whisked me into the examining room and, with a surprised look, confirmed I was pregnant. A sonogram, newly invented, showed that I was four and a half months along already.

Ron and I were in a state of shock. That night we went to a local pub, with some friends, to hear a band, and I could not stop grinning. I realized, as I sat with my hand on my belly listening to the band, that I could feel the baby kicking already.

But there were emotional complications. The more joy I felt for this baby coming, the more I missed my first. Also this was Ron's first child and my second. In order to let him have all his happiness of being a new, expectant father, I couldn't keep reminding him that I had already been through this. I stopped talking of my first pregnancy. Yet all my memories were magnified, not forgotten; I actually needed to talk about them more.

Ron's parents were thrilled at the prospect of their first grandchild. My family acted as if this were my first, which hurt because I didn't want to deny my previous baby's existence. Of course, most of the family believed this was my first. And then there were others, kind strangers, casual acquaintances. The butcher: "Ah, is this your first? Wonderful. Congratulations!" The dry cleaner: "Your first. You must be so excited." Neighbors: "Now let me tell you what to expect."

I would have to sit with them and listen, and pretend. I was thrilled about this baby, but my joy was tainted with the necessity for further deceit.

Then too, I still had doubts about my fitness to be a mother. Would my "sin" hurt my second child somehow? Was I the only ex-unwed mother to react so inappropriately? Had all the others blithely erased the fact? Was I the only one who could not?

———

We bought a dog, in defiance of all the landlords who refused to rent to people with pets or children. Wiffle was Ron's first dog, too. We moved to a flat in the Marina district of the city. Ron grew a sympathetic belly. We began Lamaze classes: "Yes, this is my first." My doctor was going to be on vacation for two weeks in October. He promised me I wouldn't deliver before he came back, although I felt in my bones he was wrong. For a week in early October there was a miserable hot spell. In the horrid heat I had only enough energy to drift in and out of sleep.

On the eighteenth of October, I was to meet a friend to go to an art and antiques auction. I called and canceled. The day was sunny and inviting, but I felt like staying home. A half hour later, I suddenly bled a little. Then a few contractions started. I walked into the baby's nursery that I had just finished decorating, a sunny room with lots of windows and yellow cotton curtains to create a pleasing light. The bassinet was lined and draped in turquoise and white checks. I sat for a long time in the white rocker we could barely afford to buy. Wiffle curled up at my feet. I rocked for a long time, soaking in the cheerfulness of the room. Everything was ready. As I anticipated this child, my heart was light and happy. I fought back an irrational terror that I would lose this baby, too. At least I *knew* it was irrational, this fear of going into the hospital and losing control of my life again. I told myself not to be stupid, that I mustn't allow these fears to ruin Ron's experience. But I had to keep reminding myself I was safe. Nobody was going to take my baby. I paced through the flat and knew this baby was going to bring me so much joy. I just had to get past this part.

With a wary eye, Wiffle followed my every move like a shadow. I had to get a grip on myself before I called Ron. A sharp pain snapped me out of it. It was late afternoon. I called Ron at his office; he was in a meeting. I apologized to his secretary and explained. Could she possibly get him to please come home? (I wondered myself at how self-effacing I was.) His secretary practically screamed: "He's out the door already."

When Ron dashed in, I again apologized for getting him out of a meeting. He gave me a strange look. My obstetrician was still on vacation so we phoned the doctor on call, and he advised us to stay home as long as possible and keep track of the contractions. While I got comfortable on the living room couch, Ron got our one clock out of the bedroom. He plugged it into the closest outlet, pulled a chair up next to the couch, propped the clock up on his own expectant belly, and—all the lights suddenly went out. There was a blackout in the whole Marina.

Ron sat back down and tried counting one potato, two potato. But that got quickly boring. Neither of us was wearing a watch. After a couple of hours I felt a sudden shift and knew it was time to go. As we left, the lights came back on.

We were put into a dimly lit labor room, much smaller than what I had remembered at Richmond Memorial. There were two beds in this room. We huddled, alone most of the time, waiting. Ron sat in a chair at the foot of the bed, twisting the tassel of the window shade. The nurse asked him to leave, so she could examine me. I got panicky when the door closed behind him. I needed Ron there.

She asked me if this was my first baby. I wanted to lie. I didn't know how important it was for them to know. Couldn't she just read my record? The medication was taking effect, making me feel slow and, when I told her briefly about my first, I felt heavy with my shame. I asked for an epidural, not realizing that it was my emotional pain I wanted to numb.

The doctor who was to deliver our baby came in to check on my progress and introduce himself. Again, Ron was asked to leave and my heart leapt in fear. My legs, completely numb from the epidural, flopped over helplessly like two beached whales as the doctor began the examination. I forced my way out of my fog. The voice I heard seemed to be coming from a distance. "The medication has stopped the progress of your labor," the doctor was saying. I told him to stop the medication. The labor got going again. Mercifully, my memories faded. I was right there, in the present, completely absorbed in this birth. When it was time to go to the delivery room, the doctor took one look at Ron and advised him to wait outside. The baby was coming quickly now. Just before I pushed him out, I heard the first cry of an infant born in the next room. And then I heard my baby's cry. Ron was suddenly there and I asked him what the baby was. A boy, he said. They gave him to me, and I held on for dear life.

I started to hiccup. The sound rippled through the sunny silence of the nursery. I smiled down at Brett, so little, only two weeks old. His eyes met mine. He was such a happy baby and much too sociable to want to go to sleep. Then, just as I expected, he hiccupped. We were so in tune that I always got the hiccups just before he did. I rubbed his tummy to ease the discomfort. To distract him, I began to read the little poems in the Hallmark *Baby Book* my mother had sent. He listened with great intensity. I came to a poem entitled "To My Baby Son" and found when I got to the end of it that it had been written by one of my old suite-mates at Winthrop College. How wonderful, I thought. How strange, too. This was the first time my past had found me in California.

Since Brett seemed to have a great deal of sociability left in him, I told him all about my friend, the poet, and what school had been like. I loved his rapt attention. And I told him about his brother and that the two of them were connected, just like I was to him, in our hearts. Someday we would meet him, and I hoped it wouldn't be upsetting and that they would feel like brothers. There was a long road to travel before then, though.

After six years of being a mother and denying the fact, I could now openly say, "I am a mother." Even though I couldn't be completely honest, this was a tremendous release, and Ron and I were happy. We had lots of great friends; I could live in the present.

But I had trouble leaving the baby, even to go to the movies. I dragged my heels about getting a baby sitter.

When Brett was eight months old, Ron wanted to go on a

second honeymoon to Hawaii. We got the most competent nurse to be with him while we were gone. He was probably in more capable hands with her than with me. Yet leaving him was unbearable. I cried on the plane, cried as the balmy breezes floated through our room at the Royal Hawaiian, cried on the gorgeous beach. It was an interminable eight days.

When we got back, Brett acted like he didn't even recognize me. Did babies so quickly forget their mothers after all? Was there then no validity to the birth bond? Did forgetting my face mean he forgot how I felt to him? Are mothers so easily replaced? Could my spiritual connection to my sons be all in my imagination?

Ron was becoming successful, and I began to volunteer on the pediatric ward of Children's Hospital once a week. On Brett's first birthday, we bought a house. We began to talk about having a second child, and soon after I was pregnant.

Brett was just under two years old. I could enjoy this pregnancy without pretending it was my first. The flashbacks this time were dimmer, too. They came again only when I became way overdue. Waiting for this baby brought back all the waiting at Seton House. I was two weeks overdue when labor started.

Ron was there this time. I went through labor and delivery without any medication. My doctor walked in just in time to catch the baby. I didn't even have to push. Kip was born looking like a little Indian with lots of black hair—like Phillip.

Ron came back in the afternoon and we stood at the nursery window looking at Kip and all the other babies. That night, Ron sneaked Brett up to see Kip through the nursery window. I wished that the baby and I could have gone on home with them, because being in the hospital was depressing me. It seemed that anything resembling Seton House or Richmond Memorial brought all the bad thoughts back, almost physically. The grieving never stopped. It only went below my threshold of awareness for periods of time. When I got out of the hospital, it subsided again.

Chapter Eleven

Brett was three and Kip almost a year old. Lego blocks were strewn all over the parquet floor in the living room. I sat on the floor in the midst of the mess, slowly picking up all the pieces, tossing them into the box. Whoever invented Legos had to be childless. Ron was downstairs putting the kids down for an early nap. I heard his footsteps on the stairs; each step seemed to be taken more slowly. I became a little wary. Wiffle waited at the top of the stairs, tail wagging.

As he stooped down to pat Wiffle and help me with the Legos, Ron, quite uncharacteristically, avoided my eyes. Something was on his mind and it was serious. I asked him what was wrong. He stopped picking up the toys, but still did not look up at me. In a grave voice, Ron said that he thought I should forget about my first son, stop talking about him and thinking about him. (Had I been obsessing out loud?) He had his own family, Ron said, and we had ours. I had two wonderful sons and I was not being fair to them, thinking about this other child, who was no longer mine anyway. He asked me to forget about ever searching for him. I listened to his words, stunned.

Did he fear that my loving Phillip left less love for Brett and Kip? Why did my love for this child seem *wrong* to everyone else? Was it wrong for him as well? Why couldn't I let go of him, stop loving him, worrying about him? Now Ron was repeating what everyone else had told me.

My first child was not his child, but he was the half-brother of his two sons. Blood does count, I thought. He is their brother. I didn't say anything but continued to pick up the toys. Finally, I suggested to Ron that he go over to the tennis club for a while. As I heard his car leaving the driveway, I felt something inside me go.

Ron had betrayed what I believed was a sacred promise. If I had had help in dealing with the past, this might not have loomed so large. This probably could have been worked out. But with everything that had gone before, it was impossible. Although it was the last thing in the world I wanted, and I could only faintly acknowledge the truth of it to myself, our marriage had just been severely damaged.

Just as the last Lego was put away, little voices came from the bottom of the steps. There had to be an invisible cord between the kids and the Lego box that alerted them when all the pieces were put away. Wiffle licked them both as they reached the top step. They grabbed a couple of books and climbed up on my lap. One of the books was *Horton Hatches the Egg*. It was about Mayzie the Lazy Bird who had laid an egg but didn't want to sit on her nest long enough to hatch it. She asked Horton the Elephant to sit on her nest, and he did, through all sorts of trials and tribulations, always saying "an elephant's faithful one hundred percent." When the egg finally hatched, it was an elephant bird. Mayzie came back to claim her baby after the work had all been done and of course could garner little sympathy from anyone, including me. Would this be how *I* would be looked upon, when I found my son?

With Kip in one arm, a bag of groceries in the other, and Brett toddling just ahead, I tried to open the door to the kitchen. If the door opened too wide, the wind would blast through the room. In spots like these on the northern California coast, summers were colder than winters. My kids played outside bundled up in winter parkas while ten minutes away, past the fog line, it was sunny and hot. We had to move.

The phone began ringing as we were halfway in the door. Brett climbed up on the chair to reach it and the wind ripped the door right out of my hand. Papers and toys and pictures began flying around the room. I put Kip on the floor and pushed the door shut.

"It's Grandma Anne," Brett said. Ron came into the kitchen and gathered the kids up for me so I could talk. There were sobs on the other end. I was terrified. Finally Mom was able to tell me what she had called to say. She and Dad were getting a divorce.

Over the years I had seen my parents grow apart, despite their valiant efforts to keep their marriage together. They were too incompatible, such different people in so many ways. There wasn't much I could do for Mom, besides let her cry. As I stared out the window at the heavy fog blowing by, I felt a terrible sense of loss. I could hardly believe this had really happened to our family. I was amazed.

Nine short years ago my parents had been so profoundly concerned about what the neighbors might think about my having a child without being married. Now it was they who were doing the unthinkable. Had they become more courageous? Or had the sixties actually altered the mores of society in less than a decade?

In the fall of 1976 we moved to a house below the fog line, and Brett began kindergarten. Our new house was nothing special, but the land was extraordinary. One side of the backyard was a redwood grove. The other side was open and sunny, with a pool. To me the best part was the creek that ran along the pool and the back of the house. The first thing we did was build a bridge across the creek to the woods up behind the redwood grove. Here, on this land, the kids could have a really magical childhood. I looked back on all the houses I had lived in during the fifties. Often there had not been one tree in the entire neighborhood. The developers always leveled all the land before building on a tract and Dad would have to begin a new lawn from seed, and plant trees we'd never see grow to maturity.

I wanted more than anything to create a happy family. In fact, we were happy much of the time. I felt I had the greatest kids in the world. But in the midst of my beautiful, normal life I often felt lonelier, crazier, and more alienated than ever. And when things were not perfect, I could not cope, even with the smallest difficulty.

One day, by accident, I found I was watching a television program about an adoptee search group. So there were adoptees out there searching, too! But I could hardly take in the information I heard, and for days afterwards, I went around in a daze. I was unable to react to it in any meaningful way.

I found a therapist so that Ron, I thought, could get *his* problems straightened out. It is always easier to think that someone else has the problem, not you. The therapist saw both of us.

Then I went for a session alone. It took several sessions before I could stop defending myself as the innocent victim. I did not know how to stand up for myself, how to ask for things in marriage or to believe that I deserved to ask. Whether Ron had expected it of me or not, I had become a doormat. Therapy helped me to feel okay about having my own individuality, without feeling guilty. But it was six months before I casually brought up the fact that I had had a baby and given him up for adoption.

As I sketched my story, I found myself watching the therapist closely. I spoke with no emotion, as if I were chatting at a garden party. Normally he was calm and professional, reflecting me back to myself. Now his eyes showed shock. It wasn't what I was telling him, it was that I hadn't told him much sooner. I knew intuitively, before he admitted it, that he couldn't help me with this one. I felt alien to myself, in a place where I had begun to know myself. I feared I was losing his respect. I was wrong.

His compassionate response was enormously helpful. He felt bad for me, for what I had gone through. I heard his outrage and forgave myself a bit. But he said he was a marital counselor and had no background to help me with this. He recommended a woman therapist. I declined to see her.

I realized that Ron had married only half of me, and that was our problem. My guilt had weakened me. My lies had undermined my integrity. Just talking about it, and seeing how the enormous authority figures of my youth had deprived me of my power to keep my baby, I had become stronger. But my sudden glory in my own individuality, my need to assert my will, gave my marriage another blow. I had not become wise enough to allow Ron to catch up with the new me before I began to demand more from him and from the world. Since I was not working and had no separate source of income, I always had to ask Ron for money. I felt like a child. My solution was to have a joint checking account. It would indicate that Ron valued my work as a mother as equal to his financial contribution to our family. In one of our sessions together with the therapist, Ron presented me with a box of checks for our joint checking account. On the decorator checks were depictions of various famous battle scenes. I loved it. There was our strength, our ability to laugh at ourselves. However, it didn't take long before I had to ask for Ron to please put some money in the joint checking account. I rebelled at the thought of being forever in such a posture.

I took up photography, made a crude darkroom for myself and taught myself black-and-white developing. The images, latent in the paper, slowly emerged in the developing tray. First the densest, darkest places, where the least light hit the negative, emerged from the pure whiteness of the paper. Then the grays filled in. The trick was to pull the image out of the tray when the blacks were their blackest and the white still pure. At the beginning, it was a thrill to get any image. Gradually, as my eye developed, I became more critical of results.

I read lots of books, anything about finding oneself. There was a relentless hunger in my searching: If I could just find the right book to tell me what I was looking for. My studies were fascinating but not satisfying. I volunteered at the kids' school, played tennis, and studied photography as much as I could.

Our marriage faltered. We separated in April 1980, after ten years. We got along much better living apart and were committed to maintaining our friendship. In September I bought a house that was old and beautiful and charming. Of course I was worried about the effect on Brett and Kip of separating them from their father. But we were still going to live nearby. Father and children would still be in contact as often as they wanted.

One Friday afternoon, when Ron came to pick up the boys for the weekend, he handed me a tiny piece of paper, a couple of lines from a magazine. I carefully unfolded the fragile piece of paper. It was an address for ALMA, a search group for adopted people. It was the group I had heard about on TV a few years earlier. We had not talked about my son for years. I looked down at the tiny scrap of paper and tears started.

I walked through the house to the kitchen and found my purse. I put that scrap of paper in the deepest, safest recess of my wallet.

Several times each day I checked and rechecked that it was still there. Each time, just before I saw it, still hidden away, a wave of panic would wash through me at the thought that I'd lost it. In three years he would be eighteen.

The rains came in early November. I was sweeping the fallen Japanese-plum leaves off the white stucco front porch when the first fine mist of rain filtered down through the great fronds of our huge palm trees. I stopped sweeping and drank in the smell of sweet rain. We had just moved in and now here was the first rain at my very own home. How glorious!

By late evening, my feelings were different. The rains were torrential and poured through a gaping hole in the downstairs bathroom, ruining the wallpaper and the carpet. After plugging that up, I flushed the toilet and that began to overflow all over the carpet I had just blotted up. I heard a weird sound under the house and realized finally that it must be the sump pump. I went into the kitchen for a glass of wine and heard a drip, drip. And then in the dining room I heard another drip, drip that was almost a splash. My new house allegedly had a new roof. But the pots began to play a mournful tune as they caught the dripping everywhere. I went upstairs and the children's bathroom ceiling had water pouring through it. Back down in the kitchen, I got another pot and poured another glass of wine.

Lots of money and time were spent patching leaks, fixing faulty wiring, repainting, repairing all the quick solutions to an old house's problems, all of which the previous owners had hidden under beautiful decorating. Finally, I had to deal with repair people, insurance companies, the world, without a phantom male presence to keep them all at bay. I had to become strong enough to deal with problems entirely on my own.

Unaware of the seriousness of the storm, the kids and I hopped into the car to drive them to their first day of school after the Christmas holidays. We rounded the bend in the road and saw a car floating down the cross street. Ron was a mile away in our old house. The creek bordering it must have been a raging river by then. But there was no way of knowing, since the phones were down and the power was out. The rest of the day we helped neighbors as we watched the water creep higher. When I let our new dog Buffy out, she had to swim to get to higher ground. Kip's cat Blackie was stuck under the house, able to stay above the water because the foundation was high enough, but for how long? After an hour of coaxing, I got him to come out.

The waters receded late that night and the next day we were

able to talk to Ron. The water had apparently come within an inch of entering the old house.

I bought my first car, negotiated for it, dealt with more insurance people. My confidence about myself was coming back. I tried unsuccessfully to return to the advertising business. Meanwhile, I took photography classes and built another darkroom in the garage. I studied journalism. Dad had once discouraged that choice of a career, not wanting his daughter hanging around cigar-smoking reporters. Newsrooms were not for genteel Southern women.

I managed a Little League baseball team, the first woman to do so in our area. My dad had always played baseball with both Bob and me, but only boys were allowed to play Little League. It had been a bitter pill for me, then. So, I wanted to be an example to girls and to Brett and Kip.

Still chasing after a nameless discontent, I eventually considered resuming therapy. I still felt at odds with a world that worshipped a sweeter, more passive, servile female. The sixties and seventies had brought all sorts of changes but women's stereotypes persisted. Was even the Virgin Mary as passive as the Holy Fathers portrayed her? I felt she must have had real fire in her soul and certainly a sense of humor. But in the litanies, there was never a reference to Our Lady of Perpetual Laughter, only Our Lady of Perpetual Sorrow.

I overcame my earlier resistance to a female therapist when I realized I actually did not trust women and myself as a woman. When I gave up my son, it was women who had facilitated it: my mother, the social worker, the nuns at the home, the nurses at the hospital. Not one woman came forth for me, expressed concern for the great female power that I was being asked to deny, keep secret, and give up. I had been outraged by this betrayal by my own sex. Women should have known better

169

what real damage they were doing to another woman. It wasn't that impossible to function in society as an unwed mother. Any one of the women that touched my life back then could have shown me another way. Why didn't they? Recognizing the source of my anger, I could stop assuming a woman was not as competent as a man to help me. I went looking for a woman that could.

Toni was the therapist of a good friend of mine. Her office was on a houseboat. I was impressed with how unconventional I was getting; I tried hard to keep my middle-class judgments at bay. Aboard the *Omphale* (named for the Greek queen whom Hercules served, dressed as a woman) was a large reception area. Toni stood at the top of a staircase and ushered me up to her tiny office. From my chair I could look out of the window across the decks of the other houseboats lined up along the Sausalito waterfront. As I observed her and we talked, I could see that Toni combined inner strength with femininity. She was the ageless mature woman who always showed up in fairy tales to help at the crossroads. She was beautiful, intelligent, had a great sense of humor and an honest knowledge of herself.

Gently, through the weeks, she led me from talking only about my outer circumstances and the people of my life to who I was as a person, inside. Wasn't I defined by the people and circumstances in my life as a mirror reflecting me back to myself? No. I could begin to know myself by how I individually reacted to people and circumstances. Then I could learn to change my reactions, and, therefore, begin to change my life.

Toni was a Jungian and worked with dreams and archetypes, particularly the feminine archetypes. Exploring myths with her challenged the cultural stereotype I had of myself and all women. Still, it was easy to forget after I left the *Omphale* and became immersed again in my ordinary life. But slowly I began to weave truth into my life. It was fragile work. I thought of Victorian women, sitting together in circles, with heads bowed over their fine lace work, duplicating the mystical spiderweb, but oblivious of their affinity with Gaia, the goddess of Earth, of generation, of life.

Each session I tried to dredge up the past week's dramas and dreams. One day I couldn't animate them enough to talk about them. Toni waited patiently. All week I had considered telling her about my son, but I thought so highly of her that I hated admitting to her what had happened to me. As I sat waiting for the words to come, my body felt creepy. Shame and guilt, penitence and self-punishment seemed to be crawling all over me. I took a deep breath that caught Toni's attention fully. Then I said, "When I was nineteen, I had a son whom I gave up for adoption."

While I tried to control my shame-ridden body, I observed Toni with an amazingly detached mind. Tears filled her eyes. I calmed down. I stared at her tears with fascination. Toni's eyes radiated enormous compassion. Telling a woman was a completely different experience from telling a man. It was harder to admit to another woman how I had violated myself.

I told her my story. I gave her the details but didn't fill in the feelings. I wasn't remotely aware of what they were anymore. My breathing was shallow and my voice high-pitched as I spoke. I watched Toni's every reaction like a foreigner observing unknown customs, trying to assimilate and survive by not making any mistakes. At times she looked appalled. At times angry. She cried several times. I hoped she didn't think me heartless for my cool recital. It was not safe for me to cry. I knew she wanted to hug me, comfort me, but I couldn't have handled that. I sat rigidly in my chair. I had lived with this condition for sixteen years. If I let my dammed-up feelings free, if I gave in to the pain of not knowing my son, what would be left in the aftermath? I could not risk instability; I could not risk losing Brett and Kip. I would die.

At the end of my story, I told Toni that I planned to search for my son when he was eighteen. She wondered why I felt I had to wait. I explained, to her astonishment, that by law adoption records in every state were sealed which made my search feel, to me, like a criminal act. I felt eighteen to be the earliest age at which I should try to find my son. At eighteen he would no longer be a minor. I could approach him directly, if need be. I would be less likely to be treated as a heedless miscreant. Or so I hoped.

"I feel that I love him so deeply," I said apologetically. "I was supposed to forget him. I don't even know him. I wouldn't know him if he passed me on the street. Yet, I feel such a need to find him. I gave him away. He has no memory, maybe no desire to know me. He's probably with a good family. I may only disrupt his life and his family's. I know I am being extraordinarily selfish wanting to find him, but I can't seem to help myself."

"Of course you can't," Toni broke into my babbling, "you're his mother!"

Sweet Jesus, what was she saying? Tears stung my eyes and I almost bolted out the door. But I sat very still and listened to Toni. She was the first human being to tell me it was okay to love my child, even though I didn't know him and had given away all legal rights to any kind of relationship with him. My sentence had been for life, like that of a first-degree murderer. This woman was offering me hope of a parole.

Embarrassed, I told her how I had maintained one link—my prayer to the Blessed Mother. This made perfect sense to Toni. She said, in fact, I should send him love whenever I felt like it, and trust that he did receive it and know it at some level. I was speechless with the most profound sense of relief and joy. A truth I had clung to almost hopelessly had been validated by another human being. Maybe I wasn't crazy after all. I gave Toni a great hug and an eternal thank you.

On my walk that evening, I let the damp, sweet green of the dense trees and pines soak into every cell of my body and cleanse it of the pain it had been holding for so long. And then I sent an enormous feeling of silent love from my heart to my son, finally sure he would receive it. I told him again how I'd always loved him, and that it was hell giving him up, that I was going to find him and to trust that I would. I told him that he had two brothers that he would love. I prayed that he and his adoptive family were healthy and happy and that he had had a better life, as the nuns had promised.

My love seemed so powerful, I hoped he wasn't driving a car at that moment.

———

January 9, 1983. This year was almost a commemorative year: the last Valentine's Day before the search, the last spring, my last birthday, the kids' last birthdays not knowing about their brother. . . .

Sometimes the year seemed interminable. It was odd, knowing how significant it was, yet seeing life go on as usual all around me, no one knowing what this year meant to me. I swung between elation and terror but kept it all bottled up.

By the end of the summer I was constantly distracted, only

half there. Sitting around a pool at a Labor Day party, surrounded by friends, I felt myself withdrawing. I was focussed
on the great, ineradicable changes that would take place in a
few months. I prayed that no one, especially Brett and Kip,
would be hurt by what I had to do. A lot of loose ends needed to
be taken care of during the countdown.

I entered the dermatologist's office and rang the bell on the sill.
The little sliding glass window opened. The nurse noted my
arrival and asked me to take a seat. I read a sign offering a free
check for melanoma, a dangerous skin cancer. Why not? I was
there to have two moles removed anyway.

The moles were easy to take off, and I was glad they were
gone. I asked the doctor to check my left knee while she was at
it. She leaned over to examine it closely. Within a half hour, the
doctor was sewing up the hole in my leg, and the chunk she had
cut from it was being sent to the best pathologist in San
Francisco. It was a melanoma. To have walked in an hour
earlier, looking forward to cosmetic surgery prompted merely
by vanity, and to now be facing . . .

The doctor was ninety-nine percent sure she had gotten all of
it, as it was at the earliest stages, but I had to wait until the next
day for the pathologist's report. Left alone to get dressed, I
looked down at my leg, shocked, angry at it. I came from a
particularly healthy family. Physical vitality was valued and
expected. I had faith that, if I took care of my body, it would stay
healthy a long time. What could I trust anymore? I felt full of
shame at this flaw, as if I had, by myself, failed our gene pool,

created something new that succeeding generations would have to deal with.

The kids were gone, playing football, when I let myself in the gate to the house. That night, propped up with pillows, a small light washing the room with a pink glow, I faced my mortality and never felt more alive.

Whenever I made important decisions I tried to weigh them from the perspective of myself in my late eighties, sitting in a rocker on the whitewashed planks of a huge sun porch. I wanted to be able to look back over my life from that chair with no regrets. In that way, I lived with death looking over my shoulder. But now, here was the black angel, and I was only thirty-seven. Why was it happening now? Was I not supposed to find Phillip? Was this punishment for getting pregnant, or for giving him up? But, I couldn't abandon Brett and Kip as I had abandoned their brother. It couldn't be my time to die.

At ten o'clock the next morning, the doctor reported that the pathologist felt one hundred percent certain that all the cancerous cells were out of me. But she asked me to get a CAT scan to be on the safe side. Within the hour, I stood facing an enormous white capsule that looked more like it belonged in the next century. I was instructed to lie down on a strip of table in front of the tunnel-like opening. Would this magical machine then rebirth me to give me another chance at not messing up my life? I felt like I was being buried alive in a sarcophagus, being strapped down in the ambulance again, the siren screaming my secret. My baby was being born and my arms could not reach out for him. I freaked. My breathing was erratic. I was whirled back out and the CAT scan technicians gave me a quick lesson in Zen breathing. Then they slid me back into the womb once again.

I was all right this time. And the verdict was good.

.　　.　　.

Despite the breakup of our marriage, I was still close to Ron's family. Ron's sister, Barbara, knew a palm reader and thought he was very talented. I decided to consult him. The man who answered the door would have looked quite comfortable behind a desk in a bank. It seemed incongruous that someone so straight-looking should be a palm reader. I sat opposite him across his antique Hitchcock writing table. The living room of his flat was huge and flooded with sunlight. His wife came in, a small child on her hip, said hello, and left for the kitchen.

He took both of my hands in his and turned them palms up. After a few moments, he began to tell me what he saw.

"Hmm," he said. "I see you recently began to enjoy classical music." (Oh come on! Had my music drifted up from my open car window into his living room?) He noticed my disbelief and then showed me the line running under my little finger that revealed my newfound love of classical music. He said the left hand showed the potential in one's life and the right what one was doing with the potential. At this point, he said, my hands were quite mismatched, that I had not been living up to the potential my left hand indicated. He saw that I would write, he said. We always became experts at our own weakness, he said. That was interesting. Then he said something that totally amazed me. He said that my hand revealed that when I was nineteen, I had sustained a huge trauma, and that I could be assured that nothing so tragic would ever happen to me again.

Chapter Twelve

January 9, 1984. My son turned eighteen. It was a Monday. I fixed the kids their breakfast in the beautiful winter light. Their cinnamon toast smelled sweet. The paper lunch bags crackled as they stuffed them into their backpacks. Bye, Mom! And the door slammed. Our dog Buffy stood with her nose pressed to the pane, steaming the glass, her tail wagging. I watched as they got their bikes from the garage and until they rounded the corner past the stop sign and were out of sight. They were off to another ordinary day of school, while I was about to set in motion a search that could turn all our lives upside down.

I sat at the table, suddenly weak. Buffy found a warm patch on the floor and curled up. I rose from the table and sat down next to her. I had last-minute nerves. Was it wrong to want to find my son? Adoption records were sealed in every state (except for Alaska and Kansas). Implicit in the laws was the certainty that a reunion between adopted child and searching mother would ruin that child's life. Certainly, many lives would be affected by this search. Did I have a right to disrupt them?

I gave Buffy a pat and pulled myself up. My purse was on the counter next to the empty Aunt Jemima French Toast box and the half-full orange juice carton. I approached it as if I were approaching a sacred relic, this same purse I had flung down the night before. Reverently, I zipped open the Italian leather and reached in for my wallet. With trembling fingers, I pulled out the little folded piece of paper that Ron had given me, which I had kept there for four years.

I carried it to the phone. I could feel my heart beating. Eighteen years began to lift from me. My whole body felt lighter. I dialed the number for ALMA (Adoptees Liberty Movement Association).

I told the stranger at the other end that my son was eighteen today and I wanted to find him, but I didn't know where to begin. She told me there was a meeting nearby that Sunday at one o'clock, their monthly meeting. I would find it valuable, she said.

What was his first word? What were his parents like? Did he know he was adopted? Where did he live? Did he want me to find him? Did he play sports? Did he have to wear braces? How were his grades? Did he have a girlfriend? Had he graduated early, was he in college? Did his parents love him? Did they explain to him that *I* had loved him when he was born? Did he believe them? The answers were coming closer.

Sunday. The meeting place was behind the hospital in Alameda. As I scanned the room, I was immensely relieved to find quite normal and nice-looking people.

It was explained to me at the door that the first half of the meeting was open to everyone. There would be speakers and people telling their reunion stories. The second half concerned actual search assistance, and I would have to join ALMA to participate. Then I would be counseled by two assistants with respect to my search. I wrote them a check for fifty dollars and joined on the spot. Before the meeting started, I wandered around, picking up literature, getting a feel for this thing. It was amazing to me that so much had been written.

The president tapped the microphone and began the meeting by quoting Florence Fisher, an adopted woman who had founded ALMA:

There is no other contract in law — apart from slavery — in which a contract made among adults can bind the child once he/she reaches majority. I say a child doesn't sign a contract to be given away and isn't bound by it.

Then the stories began. A woman in her late thirties had found her daughter within four days of beginning her search. Her daughter's adoptive mother had given her daughter the same name she had given her at birth. She had spoken on the phone with her daughter, and the experience was so powerful she felt completely overwhelmed. I could see I had wasted a lot of time feeling unique for not forgetting my son, and guilty because I couldn't.

There were updates by adoptees who had searched unsuccessfully for years, blocked by the system, their adoptive parents' fears, their own doubts. Some had been subjected to atrocities. One searcher's adoptive father had used his powerful position in government to destroy all records leading to his adopted daughter's family of origin, despite knowing how much his daughter wanted to discover her roots. There seemed to be so much fear and anger and possessiveness involved with adoption. But there were also stories of love and courage, of families accepting new members unconditionally into their lives. A tall, elegant woman in her late fifties looked twenty again as she stood next to her recently found son, who looked just like her. With her, too, was her little granddaughter. This woman had never been able to have other children. Their joy at being reunited was palpable.

As I watched them I broke down. I stopped hearing the voices. I had a strong reaction — that I was dreaming I was in the room, feeling all my pain and other people's, too. Then I returned to reality. At some point, people had gotten up and were milling around. Like a robot, I got myself up and went out into the parking lot. I stood out there until finally I could feel my body.

I forced myself to go back. Small groups were forming. Heads were bent intently over notes and letters and documents. I sought out the two women I had felt most comfortable with. They were poring over a notebook filled with meticulous notes documenting the five-year search of a woman in her late sixties who had waited for both her adoptive parents to pass away before beginning to look, for fear of hurting them. Now she was afraid she would find her birth parents both dead, too.

I marveled at a loyalty so strong that it surpassed her need to know her full identity. After all the countless hours she had spent on her search, why did she now say she wanted only to know her medical history? It was absurd. I wanted to go over and shake her into admitting her real need.

How would knowing her original family have destroyed the relationship she had had with her adoptive family? I was frightened by her loyalty to them. What if my son shut himself off out of a similar loyalty?

The woman gathered all her millions of pieces of paper and stuffed them back into her notebook. She stood up to make room for me, papers still askew, a sad look in her eyes, determination in the set of her jaw.

Sitting in her place, I looked across the Formica table at my two search assistants, Lu, the older woman with the newfound son and granddaughter, and Dolores, a woman my age. I told them I was just beginning and didn't have a clue as to where to start. They asked for details I might remember: when he was born, the name of the agency, of the home, of the hospital. I could recall none of these things except my son's date of birth. *I drew a blank on almost everything.* How could I have forgotten?

Lu said many women cannot even remember the exact day their children were born, some not even the month. So much pain has to be buried in order to go on with life that memories are buried along with the pain. The mind can't be selective when it's in a traumatic situation. Many women are actually amnesiac about that period of their lives, having only trace memories for years after. The memories surface as unaccountable depression in the months surrounding the birthday. The depressive feelings are rarely attributed to the original trauma. It was true. By this time I could not remember the names of the nurses, the nuns, or even the hospital or the name of the home for unwed mothers. It was amazing.

Lu asked me if I was married now, and I told her that I was divorced. She wasn't surprised. Women who relinquished their children often are unable to have a good marriage, she said. I didn't like the word *relinquished*. It softened the reality too much. Low self-esteem affected the chances of a good marriage, she went on. Often women who have given up a child for adoption get into a relationship with a man whose own deep pain and distress matched theirs. And the trauma of betrayal by these women's fathers and mothers, people they loved, left them unable to trust others, subjecting their marriages to this additional strain. The truth of what she was saying passed right through my body like a cold chill.

Dolores opened her notebook and showed me pictures of her son. He was a couple of months older than mine. Dolores and her son's adoptive mother were corresponding, using a social worker as an intermediary. Each month, the adoptive mother sent pictures updating Dolores chronologically from the time of his birth. She had asked Dolores to wait two more years before making direct contact, because she didn't think the boy was ready to handle the meeting. She didn't know that Dolores had known their name and address all along. Dolores looked pleased at the prospect of telling her this when the time came, at her chance to dispel one of the big myths—that birth mothers are unstable and incapable of doing what would be best for their child.

I hated the term "birth mother" right away. It sounded like we were brood mares and implied that the relationship to our children ended at birth. Dolores said that "natural mother" wasn't any good either, as that implied the adoptive mother was unnatural. The same with "real mother" and "first mother." "Biological mother" sounded so clinical.

The struggle to find a term to describe us underscored the existence of a competitive situation. Why would someone leap to the conclusion that they were *unnatural* just because someone else was termed natural? I could see how "real" could be wrong for both. First mother was no good. Second wasn't necessarily worse than first, but second was second. The lack of a good term to describe us indicates to me the effort society makes to deny or repress the fact that the child's other mother still exists after adoption.

Dolores closed her notebook and gave me instructions on

how to develop my own search record. She and Lu advised me to think about telling Brett and Kip and the rest of my family that I was actively searching now for a child I had given up for adoption. Otherwise, the kids would wonder why I was so distracted and sometimes on edge. They might blame themselves. Also, I might get an important call that I would want them to be sure to relay. There was, as well, the chance that my son was searching for me.

My heart skipped two beats. But I wasn't sure about telling my kids yet. I had to think about that one a while.

The musty smell of old books hung like fog in the stacks of the Sutro Public Library, a genealogical library in San Francisco. I sat on the floor. On my lap was a heavy leather-bound edition of the 1966 Polk Directory—a listing by street address of institutions and residents. This particular one was for Richmond, Virginia. I copied down all the names of the hospitals. Richmond Memorial rang the loudest bell after eighteen years. I looked up maternity homes. I found St. Gerard's, run by the Missionary Sisters of Verona. That didn't sound familiar, but no other Catholic home was listed. I wrote down all the Catholic churches and a few convents. Seeing all the "Saint this's" and "Saint that's" gave me the shivers. The past was coming back to haunt me.

Next I found my old hometown phone book for 1966. I looked up our old number and those of all my friends and of our favorite places. Yes, they had all existed, even if they seemed so unreal. Everything from my past seemed as if it had happened eons ago. The memories were so covered up, it was actually frightening. Even much of my childhood was difficult to recall.

For a long time I sat among the stacks, the heavy directory on my knee, and tried desperately to remember names, addresses—anything at all.

Driving home from the library, I sank deeper and deeper into depression. It felt like quicksand and I was frightened. In a panic, I called Toni when I got home. She made time to see me that night.

Toni beckoned me up to her office on the houseboat. A fire was glowing in the Franklin stove and it was comforting. I think Toni was surprised to see me in such a state. I had always been in control of myself before. Now as I sat with her, I was a pregnant, powerless teenager again, looking for help and expecting only reproaches. I was going to be exiled from my life and hidden away again. The shame of being in that home for unwed mothers made me feel like a leper. I didn't want to remember any of it; my searching was bringing it all back, and magnified. I was going to get swallowed up in it.

Toni helped me. She said that my self-respect would come back as I took charge of my life and found my son. Just like any other mother, I had to know he was okay.

The next morning, after the kids were off to school, I got out my list and found again the number for St. Gerard's Maternity Home. How to phrase my request? ALMA stressed not to mention adoption. Doors might close, not just for me, but for everyone who followed. I thought of saying I was searching for a long lost aunt who had been a nun in a home for unwed mothers. I cringed at the term "unwed mother," even though I had been one. I still may be, I'm not sure when the term ceases to apply, if it ever does.

More lies to tell after eighteen years of them. It was degrading. Lying about nuns to nuns was too much even for me. I decided to tell the truth. It was too insulting to me and my son not to. Otherwise I would be pandering to the false necessity for secrecy in the first place.

I dialed the number, fingers shaking uncontrollably. A sweet, gentle voice answered the phone. As it turned out, St. Gerard's was now a home for the aged run by the Little Sisters of the Poor. I asked her if she knew of a home for unwed mothers. She said, oh, yes. Seton House. A Sister Agatha had been in charge.

"Oh my God," I said. "Was it on Washington Avenue?" My memory had clicked.

The gentle voice at the other end said she used to crochet sweaters for the little Seton House babies seven years earlier. My breath caught as I flashed back to Mrs. Hogan helping us with our knitting in the TV room. She said Seton House had closed the previous year and the records were stored elsewhere. I gave a silent cheer.

How many records over the years? How many girls? How many babies? How many tears? Enough to fill an ocean. And Seton House was only *one* such place.

She said she would check with the Bishop to see where the records had been transferred. The Bishop! I was grateful that I had not lied. A half hour later, my phone rang. It was the same woman. She told me the telephone number for the place in which the records were now kept and wished me luck finding my son.

This time I dialed with more confidence. The woman who answered at Catholic Family and Children's Services was quite friendly and helpful, despite the fact that my search was illicit. She said that little information was left in the records but she would send me whatever there was. She also gave me the address and phone number of an agency in North Carolina that

185

had actually handled the adoptions. The main records would be there. She, too, wished me luck. ALMA had prepared me for the worst, so I was grateful for my good fortune.

As I contemplated my next call, a dark form came toward me from out of the past. Who was that social worker who used to drive up to see me from Catholic Social Services in Charlotte? I felt afraid as I tried to get her into focus. Only my desire to find my son could overcome my terror of having to talk with her again. It had been so long. She *must* have retired by now. Or they could have sent her on another mission. I still couldn't remember her name, but I was almost able to visualize her face.

I called. The secretary put me right through to a social worker, a woman named Elinor Green. I had the uncanny sensation as I spoke to her that something major was about to happen. Her voice was kind. I told her why I was calling. She said she would have to look up the records. She promised to call me back within thirty minutes. She warned me, however, that the information she could give me would be minimal. North Carolina law prohibited disclosure. If I was in one room and my son and his adoptive mother were in an adjoining room, all wanting to be reunited, she still would not be able to help us. It would be against the law.

I stayed, sitting cross-legged, on the floor after we hung up, trying to absorb the full implications of what she just said. Then I got up and stormed into the kitchen and paced around the house in outrage. I might never ever get to see my son. The lawmakers might just as well have been slave masters, cold-bloodedly arrogating to themselves the right to separate children from their mothers. Yet I felt self-doubt, too. Could they be right?

The phone was ringing. I ran and caught it on the second ring.

It was Elinor. The records were before her. My whole life was in her hands. She knew my son's name, his parents' names. She knew more about him than I did. She could legally have this information; I was not permitted to. Still, I could not get angry at her. She was only doing her job. I felt bad for her, knowing from her kind voice that she wanted to tell me more.

She said she could only give me a little bit of information from the records: There had been no contact after the first year, which was normal. The adoption was finalized in 1967. The records stated he was a happy, well-adjusted boy.

Oh, my God, she's talking about my baby.

I tried to keep my voice from cracking. My throat closed up and I couldn't speak or breathe. I heard her voice asking if I was still there. Yes, I barely managed to say.

He went to a warm and loving family. The parents were outgoing, intelligent, well educated.

I was writing down every word she uttered.

The mother was quoted as saying she felt "so fortunate, so fortunate." The baby was happy and bright. He had a hernia repair at a little under a year.

My heart wrenched. He had surgery and I wasn't there for him.

She said he had blond hair and brown eyes.

I swallowed hard. Could she tell me any more, I asked.

No, she couldn't. She advised me to register with the International Soundex Reunion Registry (P.O. Box 2312, Carson City, Nevada 89702), a "mutual consent" registry that tries to match searchers—adoptees, adoptive parents, and birth parents. She also advised me to write a letter she could place in the records, in case the North Carolina law ever changed. She said she hoped it would.

I needed to get off the telephone. I was feeling faint.

"I can't tell you any more unless there is a medical reason," I heard her say. "Then I would be required to try to find them."

My voice came out sounding like I had just sucked on a helium balloon. "Does a melanoma count?"

Yes, she was certain that counted. It counted!

I had been a split second away from hanging up on all hope. Suddenly she was under obligation to contact my son and his parents. That, too, was the law. She promised to let me know as soon as she found them. I thanked her profusely and hung up, elated.

In the state of mind I was in, I would never have been able to make up a decent lie about a medical cause which would require her to search. If I had not just recently had the melanoma, I would not have had the presence of mind to think of it. My cancer scare had actually been a gift.

I held my notes in both hands, clutched to my heart, and rocked back and forth. I stared at the paper with my scribbled notes. Happy, well-adjusted boy. Blond hair. Brown eyes. Warm, loving family. "So fortunate, so fortunate."

I was being asked to be content, to know this much about my firstborn child and perhaps no more. How could I be?

All afternoon I kept coming in and out of a dream, floating. I did have a son. It really did happen. Of course I knew it, but for eighteen years, nothing had been tangible but my tears. And they had been rare.

Sitting on the steps outside, my arms wrapped around our dog, I contemplated telling Brett and Kip. I did not want to keep this secret from them another day. The burden had become too great.

Brett was twelve, in the seventh grade. Kip was nine and in the fourth. Were they old enough to handle such news? It was one thing to have a normal fantasy about discovering an older brother. I had always wished for one. But what happens when fantasy becomes reality? And what would they think of me? Was I about to permanently damage their psyches, endanger their good relations with women, shatter the trust they had in me as their mother? Was I unfit to be *their* mother, too? My haunting fear: I might lose them, too.

Backpacks thudded, landing on the hardwood floor just inside the kitchen door. The lid of the cookie jar clattered on the counter. I walked in as the refrigerator door was slamming shut. Making my usual noises about not eating too much before dinner, I made discreet inquiries about how much homework they had to do. If they had a lot, I would not say anything.

"Not much."

Oh my God. I decided to wait until after dinner to tell them so that their blood sugar would be on my side. (Any excuse worked at this point.) How in the world was I going to do this?

I watched each morsel of food disappear from their plates with a mixture of dread and elation. With the last bit gone, Brett and Kip scraped their chairs back from the table in unison, wanting to play a little catch before the last of the daylight disappeared.

I asked them to wait. We needed to have a little family talk. Instantly, they became alert, intuitively aware something major was coming up. They stared seriously at the inane expression on my face. Whenever I was nervous, I began grinning like the village idiot. The harder I tried to gather myself into a pillar of strength and wisdom, the sillier I felt.

"Is this about the birds and the bees?" Brett asked, half-joking. Already boredom was settling on his face. What a brilliant lead-in!

"Well, yes," I said. "In a way it is all about the birds and the bees." And I told them the whole story, calmly and simply, no flourishes and no excuses.

Brett was old enough to grasp the full significance of what I was saying. Having full knowledge of and a keen seventh-grade interest in the birds and the bees, the implications were not lost on him. I must have had sex three times then. Twice with his father and once with someone he had never known. It was obvious from his expression that his first reaction was shock. And then he looked at me and said, "Mom, that must have been so awful for you."

I looked over at Kip, whose eyes were wide, and watched as the news sank in. I knew as I saw the love and compassion on their faces that this was my finest, most thrilling and rewarding moment as a mother. Nothing would ever make me so proud as their spontaneous reaction just had. Their first question was, "Do you think he could be John Elway?"

Both boys felt John Elway was the ultimate hero, as he was at that moment being wooed by both the National Football League and major league baseball teams. I said that I didn't think John Elway was adopted. Brett wanted to know when the next flight was to North Carolina. It was difficult to explain to him, with his child's open heart, that the laws would not allow us to go there and find him. I was embarrassed to tell my sons that some people thought it was wrong for them to meet their brother.

Kip wanted him to come watch him play baseball and help him with his homework. Did I think he would want to? I felt sickened having to say that there was a chance we might never meet him after all. It was one thing to discuss this with adults and another to have to tell this to trusting children.

I was horrified in a new way when I had to admit to my own

children that I had given away one of them. "Why?" they asked. Telling them I had done what was best for their brother, when I had no way of knowing and making sure it had been best, sounded hollow. It was clear from their expressions they saw through that.

Did I name him? Yes, I named him Phillip. How big was he when he was born? What was his father, Chris, like? How tall was he? Kip asked if I would love Phillip more than them, since I'd divorced their dad. I wouldn't have anticipated that question in a million years. They were relieved to know that Ron knew about him. Kip turned to Brett, bursting with a little brother's mischief. "You are not Mom's oldest!" I had never thought of that either. Brett said he had already realized it. I saw his hurt and my heart went out to him.

Satisfied for the moment, they went up to their rooms to do their homework. I didn't have the strength quite yet to get up and do the dishes. But I felt deeply peaceful, an even deeper peace than starting my search had brought. I no longer had a great lie separating me from my children. We were a true family finally.

The next night, I took the kids to dinner at McDonald's. I felt it was best to find out under the neutral protection of the golden arches how they were doing after learning about their brother. I allowed as much time as my patience could bear for them to get into their Big Macs and fries, before I casually asked, "So, what do you guys think about learning you have a big brother?" (How would Donna Reed have phrased it?)

I thought I saw a flash of hurt in Brett's eyes. "It's fine," was all he said.

Kip said, looking up, "I shared it with my class today! They thought it was great."

I could just imagine the stunned silence at thirty-some dinner tables, as the fourth-graders all over town relayed Kip's great news. My French fry stuck in my throat. I had not planned to come out of the closet quite so fast.

The next day was my turn to volunteer at the annual Hot Dog Day at school. Sean was the first to run up to me. He had been on my Little League team. "Mrs. Schaefer, I heard about your son! What is his name? When will you find him? I hope you find him soon!" Right behind him to catch the tail end of his questions were all the rest of Kip's gang of friends. One of them asked how Kip got so lucky. I told them they would all meet him whenever we found him, and tried to explain everything as simply as I could. Satisfied, they ran off to play. Their easy acceptance left me feeling that everything was going to be all right.

On my way home, driving through the tree-lined streets, I was suddenly turning the bend of Friendly Road to my old house in North Carolina, with the terrible secret that at all costs had to be kept from the neighbors. If I had actually had my baby in my arms, would we have been welcomed with compassion? Was it our own individual attitudes that created "society" or was it society's attitude that created us? How many women had abortions for the same reason we gave our babies up, when what they really wanted was to have the baby?

Every day I did a little something. I sent for hospital records, the original birth certificate, registered at the Soundex Reunion Registry, found a group in North Carolina, the Adoption Information Exchange (AIE, 8539 Monroe Road S-126, Charlotte, North Carolina 28212). I began to write the letter I wanted placed in the Soundex and North Carolina records.

Each little thing I was able to do seemed like an extraordinarily powerful act. When I mailed a letter requesting my hospital records, I saw it leaving a smoky trail clear across the country. Strangers might think these acts were wrong. But I had to go on. As I anticipated the responses, the daily highlight became the mail. My mailbox became a holy shrine, a place of power. One flip of the lid was able to make or ruin my day.

I began searching for Chris, too. I felt he should know what I was doing, and besides, he might know something, or be able to help me remember. I couldn't find him, but I found Jessica. We had not talked in years, not since Kip had been a tiny baby. She and her new husband had come to California for a visit then. Seeing her had hurt too much, brought too much of the past back, and I stopped writing. Until I began my search, I had not seen the connection. She sent me a long letter, which included Chris's address and phone number. I wondered if I could muster the courage to call him.

The next day, late in the afternoon, I sat down to make that call. It was a Friday. Chris would have the weekend in which to recover. It had been eighteen years since we had said goodbye to each other. I had heard he married shortly after I married Ron. I could smell again the sweet jasmine in the early summer evening air, see the enormous white magnolia blossoms lit up in the dark sad night, taste again the tears. Now I remembered our premonition that something had been wrong with our baby, and how I was terrified by the strength of my own wishful thinking, my hope that somehow we could get our baby back. I didn't want to remember too much—so much young love mixed up with so much piercing pain.

I dialed the number Jessica had sent, my heart pounding in my chest. I hoped my voice worked. Chris answered and the sound of his voice melted eighteen years away in an instant. I said, "Chris, it's Carol."

"Oh, my word! I am just thrilled," he said.

I told him why I was calling now. He was so happy I was doing it, because he had often thought about searching, too. In fact, he and his wife Emily had tried to take some steps, but didn't know how to go about it. I was so pleased that he had married a woman who loved him enough to love his child. I said she must be a remarkable woman. He said, "Yes, she is."

There were some funny little twists of fate. His wife had a son from a previous marriage who was a year older than our son. Chris had adopted him. He was able to feel he knew the different stages our son was going through because of his adopted son, of whom he was very proud. He had put him through the best private schools and now he was going to one of the top universities in the country, with plans to go on to law school.

We caught each other up on our lives and old friends, and tried to put what had happened in some sort of perspective. I told him only two things kept my regrets manageable, Brett and Kip. Nothing else I had done had ever made up for my son not being with me. Not all the material goods I had been blessed with, not my education, "career," or anything else. It wasn't with bitterness that I said that, and I hoped it wouldn't make him feel guilty. It was just the truth. Hopefully, we would find that our son had benefitted as the sisters had promised, even though, according to the studies I had since read, children growing up adopted were deeply affected by not knowing their original family. We just had to pray that our son hadn't suffered because of our separation.

We finally hung up after an hour and a half, with most things I really wanted to say left unsaid. I wouldn't have known where to begin. He had become a really wonderful man, I thought. He promised to write a letter for the records and to help with the search in any way he could. I sat in the same spot for over an hour after hanging up, staring at the phone. This search was releasing powerful emotions, almost more than I could handle. But it meant a great deal to me to know that Chris had not forgotten our child.

I watched Brett and Kip career their dirt bikes around the corner and skid onto the driveway. Thank God for them. I got up from my reverie, starting dinner before the kitchen door burst open. I told my boys that I had talked with Chris, glad to be able to tell them he was a caring man.

After dinner, on his way to the TV room, Kip paused and asked what would happen if Phillip was a nerd and we didn't like him. In fact, he went on, he probably *was* a nerd and he was *sure* he wouldn't like him. Brett said he wondered that, too. I sat down drained, angry that my sense of humor had abandoned me when I needed it most.

———

No one could possibly imagine my powerful, raw, skinned-alive feelings without experiencing the situation personally. Friends were frustrated trying to give me support. They pointed out to me all I had to be grateful for. I didn't need to be told what I already knew. Philosophical statements like "things always work out for the best," or "how they were meant to," did little to salve my spirit, and merely added to my guilt. The only real understanding came from those who had walked in the same path. But, so little research had been done, we were like the blind leading the blind.

I saw that my search triggered a lot of pain for women who had had abortions. At least I might find my child; their loss was permanent. But they had somehow been able to mourn their terrible loss and get on with their lives. I couldn't ever let go of the past, didn't want to, and couldn't if I did. In one of the newsletters I had subscribed to, there was an article by a woman who had lost a child through death and one through adoption. She said she could grieve for the loss of her dead child, but her grief for the child she'd given up was inconsolable. Another had told of a life filled with abuse and death, all of which she could deal with. But of everything she had experienced, not being with the child she gave up was by far the worst. When I read those stories, I finally stopped wondering if I was crazy.

Toni had worked hard with me, helping me to see my rights and to honor my relationship with my first son. No longer ashamed about what had happened, I was able to tell friends pretty comfortably. To my shock, though, I lost a few of them. Men were more likely than women to have a negative reaction: My rights had ended when I signed the papers, was their attitude. I should have put the past away and forgotten the child.

Women often showed more sympathy. But if someone had an adopted member of their family, they would look at me with fear as I told them of my search. Their horror at the thought of mothers searching for *their* adopted family members completely blotted out who I was. Suddenly they were frightened of me, and I would become afraid that my own son's family would react like that.

Chapter Thirteen

I returned home from a whole day in San Francisco. Ron had picked the children up for the weekend, and my friend Janie and I were going to see a play a little later that night. As I walked up the steps to the kitchen door, I resolved to go into the city more often. The change was good for me. To keep the spell intact, I turned on only one soft light in the living room, as I flipped through the mail.

There was a letter from Catholic Social Services and also one from Chris. I stared at both envelopes, paralyzed. Elinor, the social worker, must have had some news of my son. This letter was the first physical evidence of my son I'd had since I last held him and whispered goodbye. How incredible that Chris's letter would arrive on the same day. I gripped both and clutched them to me, afraid they would vanish into thin air before I could read them, afraid of what they might say.

I wanted to hold onto my hopes and dreams and fantasies a little longer before reading the truth. I got up from the hearth in the living room where I had been sitting, walked into the kitchen and called Janie to see if she could come over a little earlier before the play. I wasn't sure what shape I would be in after reading the letters. I might need her. Then I sat back down on the hearth and opened Elinor's letter first.

She had written it on Valentine's Day.

Dear Mrs. Schaefer,

I am happy to be able to tell you that I have located your birth son. I have spoken with his mother. Your birth son has fair sensitive skin and, as he is out of doors a good deal, his mother appreciated the warning about your susceptibility to skin cancer.

I gathered, from our conversation, that she was a warm, accepting mature person. She feels confident about her relationship with her son. She told me he had not raised many questions about his heritage or his natural parents, but I think she will be supportive of him should he decide to question or search.

His mother described him as a handsome young man. He has brown, curly hair. He is a good student and all-around athlete. He is talented in art and interested in psychology. He appears to be warm, loving, and secure, and she said that he feels good about himself and his family.

I hope this information will be helpful to you. According to the laws of our state, I can share no more. Thank you for your concern and for allowing us to pass on the medical information.

Sincerely,
Elinor Green

He was all right. He was just as I had always imagined him. Thank God. He sounded like a normal kid. Was his hair as curly as Chris's or more wavy like my mother's? The words lifted off the page and I felt I knew him somehow, could feel what he was like. "Your birth son," she wrote. What did that mean? His mother? Her son? His family? Feels good about his family . . .

Not many questions about his heritage . . . He must not have inherited my curiosity; I would have a million questions. I must not let myself feel hurt. What else had she written — warm, loving, a secure young man who feels good about himself and his family. Perhaps I should stop searching. I might mess up this great life. He might not want or need me in it. He had few questions. The one thing he knew about me now was that I could give him cancer. How charming. What must he think of his "birth family"? How would he imagine me now? Couldn't Elinor have called him and told him I loved him, had always thought about him, prayed for him? Thank God he was fine!

The next morning, I made ten copies of Elinor's letter. One I sent off to Chris. The others I put in various special places in case a disaster happened and one got destroyed. The irony was not lost on me. How compulsive I was about a mere letter, when eighteen years before I had given away a baby.

The thrill of the letter was beginning to fade. The little bit of knowledge about my son in no way satisfied my great hunger to know him. I knew the reaction I was supposed to have was gratitude. But how could a one paragraph description salve a mother's yearning for her child?

To calm myself, I gathered together the negatives I had developed for my photography class and went into my crude darkroom in the garage to make prints. The images emerging from nothing, created by light, held enough fascination to match the churnings and stirrings within me. When I came out of the darkroom, the sun had long set and the air was quite cold.

I looked up at the house. No lights were on and Buffy and the cats hung around their dishes piteously, letting me know it was long past their dinner. I filled their bowls and began to clean the darkroom and wash the prints.

I had to think about telling my parents. I would call Dad and write Mom. I knew Dad would support anything I did, or at least my right to do it. After my parents' divorce, I had had an opportunity to talk with Dad about the past, mostly about the fact that Ron already knew. It had shocked him to learn that I had told Ron from the outset. He was still living in a time when such things were kept in the closet. He had been afraid for me all those years, worrying about someone finding out. And then what? Would they behead me? Burn me at the stake? Ostracize me at PTA meetings? I know he felt forever grateful to Ron, after that, for marrying me anyway.

Mom and I had never talked about "it." I felt our relationship was terribly strained. She always wondered why I never wrote, didn't call enough. I wondered, too. I was always angry with her, but had suppressed the reasons. Even in therapy, I never connected my anger with having to give up my son; I always blamed that on myself. I knew she was hurt and puzzled by my coldness toward her, but I couldn't change it. I would write her to say I was searching. I was afraid of her anger at my putting the family in jeopardy in the neighbors' eyes once more. There was also a risk she would never speak to me again. But I would not give up my quest now.

I tried for maturity, beating back the anger that raged up in me. I didn't want to feel it. But I wished I didn't have to tell her. I wished my search could be *my* secret so I could keep my son this time. But then I thought, what if my son were searching for me and called her? I had to alert her. And we all had to get our act together before I found him.

The next morning I called Dad. Brett had had a *Roots* project in school the previous year and Dad had done a great deal of research for him. He'd found the boys were the twelfth generation to be born in the United States, and that the family could be traced through four Scottish kings, through Isabel, mother of Robert Bruce, to a baron who had signed the Magna Carta. He told me now that he hoped that someday my first son would be able to know his lineage.

What would it be like for someone who had had his roots completely severed? Did knowing matter to everyone or was it an individual need, a personality quirk? How much would it matter to my son?

Buoyed by my conversation with Dad, I sat down to write Mom. I kept the letter simple. After mailing it, I called my sister Janice. I needed her best guess about how Mom would react. When I told Janice about my baby, I was shocked to learn that she had always known. She had been suspicious when things had become strained at home, and I was no longer allowed to see Chris. Then, at Joanie's wedding, she overheard the battle of the girdles, and knew for sure. How deep did the psychological wound go for her, a fifteen-year-old witnessing her sister banished for being pregnant and coming back without her baby? The most domestic of any of us, she had never had children. She had had no one to talk to about this, since it was such a secret, and our parents assumed she didn't know. Did she subconsciously believe that if she had a child, it would disappear into the deep, dark woods, captured by wicked witches? How deeply do secrets affect all of us? My brother never had children either. Although he swore he didn't have a clue about what was happening, did he, deep down in his soul? And what about my sister Ellen, only four and a half years old at my son's birth? My son could be like a brother to her. She has not had children either. Was the strain of our secret the reason my parents' marriage didn't last? How eroding were secrets in a family?

All week I wondered about the response Mom would have to my news. I figured that, after a while, she would write me back a cautious letter, one I would have to read between the lines. Instead, she called. She had just read my letter. She was thrilled that I was searching. I wanted to sit down, but I couldn't stop pacing around the kitchen, the phone tight against my ear.

She was beside herself with excitement about what I was doing. Three years before, in fact, she had a strong urge to search herself. That was odd. So had Chris wanted to search three years before. A little tendril of fear clutched at my throat. Had there been some reason in my son's life that had triggered this need? I told her I had talked with Chris and she was thrilled all over again. I would not have dared mention Chris's name to my father. Then she said she had always believed Chris and I would have made it if we had gotten married.

I was stunned. Had my brain warped over the years? Was it warped when I gave up my baby? Had all this been merely a miscommunication?

"You know," she said, "I saved a little Christmas ornament that was with your things when you came back from the home. I hung the ornament on the tree every year in the baby's honor. I always wondered if you had noticed it."

I asked her what it looked like. I didn't have the faintest recollection of it. But along with my shock came complete relief, and happiness. Her joy was genuine.

We talked a little while longer, but then I had to get off. I was exhausted. The phone had barely landed back down on the receiver, when I was hit by a torrent of anger. At first, I felt guilty about the anger and puzzled as to why I was feeling it. I couldn't have asked for a lovelier response from my mother. But then I recalled the little ornament, hung from the tree every year. How could she make such a ritual of the ornament, yet never ask me how *I* felt not having my child with me, never think about the pain *I* might be feeling, wondering where he was for Christmas, never mention how sad the memories of that first Christmas must have been for me. Yet she did it with an innocent heart, I knew. She only did what she—all of them— thought would be best. Her whole generation had a superhuman ability to bury their feelings and painful memories, and there were some things they just didn't know, and didn't want to find out, about the human heart.

Tomorrow I would try again to find my child.

I had been told it was important to find a group located as close as possible to where my son's adoption took place, in order to have the best chances of working around the system. I contacted Adoption Information Exchange in North Carolina. Like adoption groups throughout the country, AIE provides support groups, publishes a monthly newsletter, and assists with searches. It is also politically active in the state.

As it happened, Grace, the president of AIE, knew Elinor Green well. They had been on local talk shows together. She assured me that Elinor was very open to reunions. Grace promised to search for me and to send me a list of names, one of which would be my son's name. She could narrow the field, but, like most searchers, she wouldn't tell me how she'd get the list, for fear disclosure would prompt officials to close off access to the information. I realized I was plugging into an underground network that was working to get around a rigid system.

Grace asked me to give her a couple of weeks. She would call as soon as she had the list. This was the third week in February.

A month passed. I did not hear from Grace. Unfortunately, adoption search volunteers also have regular jobs and their own families. I knew Grace was doing her best, but it was impossible for me to wait. I telephoned her again. In her Southern drawl, she explained she had lots of news, but no names. Elinor had spoken with her about my search and had asked her to wait until after my son's graduation to release any information to me. The summer would be a less disruptive time for him. Grace had received a clear impression that Elinor was using my search as a test case, feeling, from talking with both mothers, that our reunion would be successful if any could be. Suddenly, I felt a tremendous responsibility. Many lives might be affected by the outcome of my search. I was more than ever determined to have it be successful. But I begged Grace to do the record check now anyway, in case anything happened in the future to prevent her from getting the names.

I wept as I hung up the phone. It was hard to understand that I could have a negative effect on my son; I only wanted him to be happy. Unconsciously, I rubbed my belly, remembering him. It seemed impossible to think I could not watch him graduate for fear I might mar the day for him. Why did people assume we unwed mothers were so unloving, so insensitive, so rapacious? Did they deep down feel we had to be; did they despise us because we had given up our babies in the first place?

My hospital records arrived the next day. But the pain they brought back was too much to handle, except in small doses. Each time I could go through another item, I felt stronger, more centered, remembering how brave I had been back then. If I breathed too deeply, I was back there. I controlled my memory with shallow breaths. *Breath. Prana. Life.*

The Seton House records were enclosed as well. I had gained

only six and a half pounds during my pregnancy and actually lost four of them while I was there. My doctor, now, would be shocked to know that. I scanned the forms to see if any concern was noted. The only comment repeated every week was "no complaints." Such a good girl I was. I saw that we had taken water pills. I had forgotten all about those and the obsession about too much water weight. I remembered the weekly visits, sitting all together in the small room. I remembered the excitement of seeing the doctor, someone from the outside world.

———

The first week of March I sent a letter to my son. It would be forwarded to him by Elinor.

It had been an awkward letter to write, because I could not have anything in it that might be considered identifying—no places, no names, no specific physical descriptions. And I didn't know the name by which to greet him. I had begun the letter with, "I know from talking to adoptees that they have a strong need to know their natural heritage and the circumstances surrounding their relinquishment. I will try to provide that for you within the restrictions of the law. Before anything though, I want you to know you have been in my heart every day of your life." I wondered if they would keep that last sentence in.

I described my family and told him about his roots, the information that Dad had wanted him to have. In case he wasn't interested in meeting us, I wanted him to know as much about us as possible.

A month passed, then nearly two. At the end of April, I called Elinor to see if there had been any response. Yes. Phillip (she used the name I had given him) and his mother wanted the letter forwarded, she had recently learned. And he wanted a picture.

Elinor had sent the letter but they wouldn't have received it yet. He had wanted to know if I wanted a picture. (Do the birds want to sing?) But then Elinor told me that he didn't want to meet me. He wanted to go slow.

That hurt, but I could understand perfectly. His apprehensions had to be different from mine. And it was something wonderful just to be actually in touch with each other, even through a go-between. I knew that what Elinor was doing was unprecedented for her agency. She was really sticking her neck out for us. I felt a great responsibility to make this work.

I called Chris to let him know the progress. We tried not to feel ludicrous at the strange necessity of having to speculate about what our own flesh-and-blood child looked like.

Then a letter came from Elinor. My son and his family had been sent the nonidentifying information. She had had to edit some of it, to her regret. Regrettably, too, she had to tell me that she could not be a conduit for our pictures. My son and his parents would have to get in touch with me now through the Soundex Reunion Registry if they wanted further contact. She ended her letter with the hope that I would be granted the grace and patience to maintain my equilibrium while Phillip was making his journey.

Was everyone in the world more mature than I? Why had God not granted me grace and patience? Or was it the agency asking for patience, and God wanted me to go for it?

Grace called. She was sending a list of ten names. Her search had been difficult because she couldn't match one piece of information with any of the possibilities. She felt she had hit a stone wall. She offered her best guess for which name of the ten she thought I should try first. The child's name was Paul.

Three long days and nights later, the names arrived. There was no Phillip on the list. I knew my son's present name was one of the ten on the list. But which one? Some of the names I could eliminate, as they were not Scottish, Irish, or English, and Sister Dominic had made such a point of making a perfect ethnic match.

I tried to force myself to believe that the name Paul that Grace had a hunch about was my son, but I had a feeling it wasn't. The last name on the list intrigued me the most. Grace had added it at the last minute: John Aloysius Ryan III. But would someone name a child "the third" when they were adopted? A thirty-five-year-old adopted man in one of the group meetings I had attended had talked about being "Junior" to a father who was half his size and as much unlike him as night and day. Yet he had to pretend it felt normal and right. Could this really be my son? What had made Grace hesitate to add him to her list?

I recalled a story from someone in ALMA who had said each time she ran her finger down her list of sixty possible names, the hair on the back of her arm stood on end when she passed a certain one halfway down. Nonetheless, she methodically went in alphabetical order. She found her son was the thirty-fifth name, the same name that had triggered her chill. Was my interest in John Aloysius Ryan III meaningful or irrational?

At this point, I became completely consumed with the search. No one around me, except those involved with adoption themselves, could understand my obsession. I decided to focus all my energy on tracking down Grace's hunch.

My imagination got to work formulating an image of this

young man from the information I had: his name and his hometown. It was a little "hick" town in North Carolina, and I was concerned that he had been brought up so conservatively that we wouldn't be able to relate to each other, and that his parents would be too afraid to let us meet each other. What impact would his upbringing have on his genes? Would my being divorced confirm their picture of me as a wanton woman? All my imperfections seemed awful as I imagined his perfect parents. Did I need to return to the Church to receive absolution before meeting them? Surely they were normal human beings. What was I measuring myself against?

And why hadn't I heard from the Soundex Reunion Registry? Had my son and his parents changed their minds about wanting to correspond? As each day passed and they did not call or write, I struggled to understand their position with all my might. He was *their* son. After eighteen years, the truth that another woman had given birth to him must have faded. I imagined they barely remembered, anymore. My reappearance must have been a shock.

I needed to know his name. Then I could wait as long as he needed me to. Maybe it was the melanoma that made me fear not having the time to get to know him. Life seemed too precarious for too much patience. What if something happened to *him*? I couldn't bear to think about it.

Chapter Fourteen

I needed a break, or I would have a breakdown. Praying for a call, waiting for a letter, hoping for his name, trying to hold myself together for Brett and Kip, my heart breaking afresh every single day no news came—it had taken its toll. I hadn't gotten to see him graduate, as I had dreamed I would, but my heart wasn't breaking over just missing his graduation. It was having missed his first smile, his first steps, his first tooth, his first words, his first day of school, seeing how he was to his friends, feeding him, nursing him, loving him.

Fortunately all the pieces fell into place for a trip to Europe. That might be far enough from my phone and mailbox to restore my equilibrium. And maybe, when I returned, my son's name would await me.

Just before my departure a friend told me about a man who was said to be a wonderful clairvoyant. Perhaps the celestial realms would reveal more to me about my son than the material world had been willing to. I was more than willing to grasp at straws.

I followed Yvonne on the steep path that wound up the hill through redwood trees to John's house. We climbed the steps up to an attractive house. John seemed more like a jolly elf than a wizard. While Yvonne had her reading with John, I sat in a comfortable chair by the piano. As I contemplated asking about my son, I felt a little embarrassed and wondered if he would think me a bad person.

When it was my turn, I followed John and sat with him in front of a huge window that framed a beautiful rose garden and a hill leading up to a grove of redwood trees. I was much more excited than nervous. And very curious. John talked a bit to help me feel more relaxed. He explained that he did not read my mind. He sought answers in what he called the "divine mind." John asked me if I wanted a tape of the reading. I did. John asked what questions I had. I took a deep breath and told him I had given up my first child for adoption and I was searching for him. I had a name in mind, the one Grace was sure of. What did he think?

"Is he south of here? What I got were big letters, 'South.'"

I was blown away. "In the South," I said. He was born in Virginia. I had grown up in North Carolina.

John continued, "It seems he has school heavily on his mind. He appears to have been raised very nicely. Not southern conservative. It doesn't look like he was raised narrow-minded. He has had good chances, a good upbringing."

I felt he was right. Or I hoped so. "Will he meet his father, Chris, first, since he is living closer to my son?" I asked.

"No. He'll meet you first." It seemed unlikely. He would have to come three thousand miles to meet me first.

"Will his parents be resistant?" I asked.

"No, it doesn't look like they will be. If they aren't secure by now about their relationship, they never will be."

That, of course, made sense and actually confirmed what Elinor had reported.

I asked him if he saw me moving. He said he saw a great big gold star just north of San Diego and that when I went there, it would be to see someone who would be in my life for the rest of my life. He didn't see it necessarily as a romantic relationship. He also saw that I would be spending time in the Fresno/Bakersfield area.

I didn't have any affinity for that area, but I did have a liking for the Los Angeles beach communities: Long Beach and Redondo Beach. Maybe that was it, I thought. He said he saw me dealing a lot with programming regarding Catholic guilt. That didn't make any sense, as I believed I had already dealt with my Catholic guilt.

We ended the session with a "healing of energies," something I had never experienced before. I felt silly as he walked around, moving his hands in the air in response to energies I couldn't see. But I felt like a million dollars. When I got home and saw myself in the mirror, I looked like I had had a face-lift.

———

Ron's sister, Barbara, met me in Rome. Within two hours, I was riding on the back of her Vespa, wondering how much longer I would have my kneecaps before they were whacked off by some crazy motorist. Barbara's apartment was in the ancient city. The Colosseum was a block up the street. After a few days we left for Siena. Barbara and I traveled together until Florence, and from there to Venice. I would travel on alone to Innsbruck, Salzburg, and Zurich, then through France, and back to Rome.

With an hour to go before I was to have dinner in Zurich

with a couple I'd met on the train from Salzburg, I decided to call home. There were no phones in the room. The call had to be put through at the switchboard in the lobby. The switchboard looked like a collector's item. There was only one small light for the whole board. I wondered if they would be able to get through. Bells from the church across the street rang the quarter-hour, and then Kip answered. He was at home with Ron's mother, who was taking care of our children while I was gone. Everyone sounded fine and everything was under control. Then Kip said there was a letter from Virginia, and put his grandmother on the phone. My body became deathly still. I asked her to open it and read it.

It was a follow-up on an inquiry Grace had undertaken for me, about Paul, the name out of the list of ten possibilities she had thought most likely to be my son. On the bottom was a notation that this child had died at the age of seven. I felt sick.

Kip got back on the phone and asked me what it meant. I tried to explain; it was hard. He was distressed, too.

It was a terrible shock. I trudged wearily up the wide stairs, past the antiques, along the landings to my room on the third floor. I sat on the edge of the old feather bed, staring out the dormer window, over the river and over the rooftops. The sun was just setting behind the city. I had thought about this boy, Paul, and his family. I had been hopeful that he might be the baby I had borne. Now I was relieved that he was not, relieved that I had been assured already by Elinor that my son was alive and well. But I was still upset. I was sure his first mother, too, had thought of him every day of her life. She might never know he had been dead all these years, unless she searched for him. No one would have thought to inform her. (Did they believe she had forgotten? That she was better off not knowing?)

It could have happened to me, just as well. I wondered what

she had been doing on the day he died. Did she collapse, completely drained from a sorrow she could not name? My heart went out to his adoptive parents. Before leaving for Paris the next day, I stopped in a church and lit a candle for Paul, as much a stranger to me as my own son in a way, but now connected to me, too.

On my fourth day in Paris, I walked from the Moulin Rouge through the narrow, winding streets, past the little shops and cafés to a square at the top, with artists painting portraits of tourists. At the very top was Sacré Coeur, the Church of the Sacred Heart. My withdrawal from the Catholic Church had never diminished my appreciation for the churches themselves. Despite their magnificence, none, save the Byzantine church in Siena, spoke to me. I couldn't sense a sacredness in them. Siena's church at least had a certain humor.

Sacré Coeur was not half as grand as some I had visited. Yet, I was moved by a sudden peace as I walked through the doors. I actually blessed myself with holy water, perhaps for the first time sincerely. I walked down the center aisle and slid into a pew about halfway to the altar. Beside me was a pamphlet, which I picked up and read. It told of the church's one hundred years of perpetual devotion. There was a word I had not heard in a long time. Images of silent nuns, walking measured steps down long, cold convent halls, fingering their rosaries and murmuring their prayers emerged from the mists. I saw a group of tourists at the back of the altar. My curiosity overcame my fatigue and I rose from the pew and followed them. The light in the church was bright until I rounded the bend at the back of the altar. There I saw a number of people huddled around a great statue of the Blessed Mother, surrounded by a sea of votive candles.

She was gazing down at them, her arms outstretched,

seemingly radiating infinite compassion and solace. As I studied the statue, I wondered what made it seem so vital, so
different from Her other statues. It seemed She could step down
from her pedestal and lift up one of the supplicants at any
moment. Some of them looked at the statue like She already
had.

I approached slowly, taking in the whole scene. At a distance
of six feet, I felt like I walked into a wall of thick air. The
deepest pain from the loss of my son seemed to burst from me,
and I started to cry. At the same time, it seemed Her outstretched arms had parted a curtain in front of me and for a
split second, I saw my son standing before me. He was so real, it
was as if I could touch him. At least, it felt like it was he,
although I did not know what he looked like.

I felt enormously comforted. I lit a candle, then sat down and
let the tears come. These were the tears I had been running
from. Here was the peace that would salve my wounds.

My last night in Paris I had dinner with a woman I had met
on the train from Venice to Austria. At the adjoining table, two
men were trying to capture our attention and we let them. One
said he was a Swiss banker. The other was dark, with deep
brown eyes and a brooding quality about him. He was a painter
from Yugoslavia who owned a gallery on the Ile de la Cité. He
spoke little English.

I had made a wish that before I left Paris I would get to see
the city lights at night. As a single woman traveling alone, I did
not have the courage to be out that late by myself. So we
accepted their invitation and, after dinner, we all piled into the
banker's car and went for a ride through the city, ending up
back at the gallery. The owner anxiously wanted to read the
tarot cards for us, as if he couldn't relax until he did. The others
went first. When it was my turn, I had to listen carefully to

understand him, since his English was not good. Since we could barely communicate, he knew nothing about me.

The candlelight danced on his face as he shuffled the deck. He laid down the cards, shook his head, and picked them all back up. Again, he shuffled, laid them down, shook his head, and picked them all back up. The third time he laid them down, he sighed with resignation. He pointed to a jack and said the same card kept coming up all three times, making no sense to him. Did I have a son who was maybe twenty years old who was apart from me in some way? Slowly, I let out my stunned breath and whispered "yes."

I had just gotten home from Europe. The kids were playing baseball outside. Buffy stood on the top step, tail wagging, watching their ball. The phone rang.

I jumped, as I always did now whenever the phone rang, hoping. It was my mother calling. My sister Janice was in the hospital in Georgia as a result of neglected stomach ulcers and on 100 percent life support. The doctors didn't think she would make it through the day. In one hour I was on my way to the airport. The last thing I did was to mail a request to the State of Virginia for the birth certificate of John Aloysius Ryan III, the last name on the list Grace had sent. She had noted after it that there was something odd about its placement on the record and maybe we should ignore it. But it was the name on the list that seemed to jump out at me. So, now that I knew Paul was not right, this was the next lead I had chosen to pursue.

We all arrived at the Atlanta airport—my youngest sister, my brother and his wife—and found each other within ten minutes. Together we rushed to the intensive care unit. Mom was sitting in a chair saying a novena when we found her. The doctors were going to allow us to see Janice for five minutes. They were amazed she was still alive.

Our first glimpse of her was through the large windows. The sound of the respirator, breathing in and then collapsing, greeted us. It was a horrifying sight. She looked dead already. Bob and Ellen and I stood around her bed, and felt the great strength and love we shared as a family that ordinary life never fully revealed. It seemed to me that Janice knew we were there. She was given a 5 percent chance of making it, the estimate really a kindness to the family.

Ellen and I spent the night sleeping in chairs in the reception area. Janice was still alive the next morning. Dad and his wife, Lucy, arrived the next afternoon. We were all together for the first time since my wedding fourteen years earlier. More than any of us, Janice would have loved seeing us all together.

She held on by the finest thread for a week. Ellen and I spent every night sleeping in the reception room. Families and patients came and went. The doctors could find no treatment to pull Janice out of her near-death condition. Her blood pressure and heart rate hovered at dangerous levels. We took turns being with her for five minutes each hour. As we talked to keep her company, it became evident that there was no coincidence between certain topics and the elevation and lowering of her heart rate and blood pressure. She could hear us and respond. But at the end of a week and a half, with no signs of real improvement, the doctors felt they should operate. That afternoon, Ellen and I went to see her. Ellen held her right hand. I held her left.

It came to me to ask Janice to release all her reasons for not wanting to live through her hand into mine. I told her I could handle it, to release it all into me. As I looked down at her, feeling a powerful love, I asked her over and over to release her reasons for not getting better. Then, suddenly, she seemed so ugly that I found myself looking at her with disgust. It dawned on me that she had released her self-hatred into me. She had done it. I thanked her and told her she never would have those feelings again. Through sheer willpower, I changed her feelings in my body. Ellen was right there like a lightning rod. We both could see something had happened, but nothing we had ever heard about. It seemed we were conducting powerful supernatural energy. Janice's blood pressure and heart rate dropped. There was no way to describe to a doctor what had just happened.

That evening, in the darkened, hushed halls, we all lined up to watch Janice wheeled past us to surgery, still in a coma, still on 100 percent life support.

Ellen and I played cards. Mom said her novena. Bob and Jeri and Janice's husband Charles sat together. But not one of us talked about how we were feeling. An hour and a half went by. Then from down the hall we heard the elevator open and the gurney rattle and click-click over the linoleum cracks. She was still alive. The surgery had not been necessary.

The next day her vital signs stabilized. I felt confident enough to leave the hospital without worrying something would happen. I went to Mom's, took a dreamless nap, and then a long, hot bath.

I called home, desperate to hear the kids' voices. Ron's mother answered and said all was fine, and, oh, another letter had arrived from Virginia. She asked Kip to go get it.

Kip picked up the extension and I asked him to go ahead and open the letter and read what it said. The sunshine had not yet made its way into the room. I sat in the dark stillness. I was barely breathing. I could hear the envelope close to the receiver as Kip ripped it open. He said it was a birth certificate.

What was the name on it?

"John Aloysius Ryan III."

What was the date of birth?

"January 9, 1966."

Did it give a time?

"9:51 P.M."

"Kip, that is your brother's name. I am so glad you were the one to tell me," I said, crying. "Please give it to your grandmother. I need her to look at it, too."

Ron's mother got on the phone and read me all the information on the certificate. I now knew his parents' names, occupations, and place of birth. They were from New York, which really surprised me. His mother was eight years older than me, his father eleven. My son was the third generation son to bear the name of John Aloysius Ryan.

So my son's name was John. As soon as I hung up, I called Chris with the news. I was beside myself and could barely get the words out. He calmed me down. I could hear the relief in his voice.

I returned to the hospital on a cloud. My son's name was John. It was such a relief just to be able to say his name. John— Aloysius—Ryan. Sister Dominic had certainly found an *Irish* family. And it was a family from the North, as we had been. His father had been a captain in the Marines. Surely he would have served in Vietnam. Despite the paucity of information I had, I started to create a story.

Before I told anyone, I wanted to tell Janice. She might die before they got to meet each other, I realized. Of course, anything could happen to any of us. That was part of my urgency.

Ellen and I went in together to see her. The nurses had opened the blinds and the sun was pouring in. They had elevated her bed and placed it by the window so the sunlight spilled over the top of her bed and onto her head. The respirator was quiet. She was now breathing on her own 20 percent of the time. She seemed peaceful, so I felt it was all right to tell her. I felt she would hear on some level.

"Janice," I said. "I have some wonderful news to tell you. I know my son's name. I just found out today. It's John Aloysius Ryan III."

As if she had just had a beatific vision, her whole face lit up in the most beautiful smile I had ever seen. She turned in the direction of my voice, her eyes, still vacant from the drugs, searching for my face. I looked up at Ellen, who was doubly astonished, first at my news and then at Janice's response, her first response since she'd come to the hospital in a coma.

I had slept in a hospital every night for more than two weeks, and I was drained. Janice was getting off the life support completely in the afternoon. My flight left too soon for me to be able to see her completely free from the respirator, but I left knowing she was going to be fine.

I had never been away from Brett and Kip so long. When I finally dropped my bags on the kitchen floor, I wanted to collapse, but everything needed doing at once. After the kids went off to play with their friends, I warily eyed the huge stack of mail. Had my son written? Was there a warrant out for me for obtaining his birth certificate? All I knew for sure was that his birth certificate was somewhere in the stack.

No warrants. No letters from my son or his family. Nothing from the Soundex Reunion Registry. But there was the birth certificate. I opened the final envelope, from the Common-wealth of Virginia. Seeing a different name on his birth certifi-cate than the one I had given him, yet the same date of birth, the same time of birth, the same hospital, the same doctor's name, was bizarre. Under "full name of mother" was another woman's name. It was as if she were the one who had given birth, not me. But she had not signed the certificate on the line that asked for signature of mother. Her name was typed in the space instead.

Would it seem strange for John to look at this certificate that severed him so completely from his roots, and pretend it didn't matter, that it told the truth about him? Why couldn't the certificate state unashamedly and with great pride that this family was created by adoption, not birth, and that she was his *adoptive* mother? Why was pretending necessary?

Her relationship as his parent was one I could never have. I would never dare to pretend to be his parent. That was a privilege I could not have and a loss I would always mourn. But I had given birth to him. I had never stopped loving him. I was his mother, too, and shouldn't be wiped out of his life as if I had never existed.

This was the summer of the 1984 Olympics, which were held in Los Angeles. I had missed most of the Games. In the spring, in one of my conversations with Elinor the social worker, she had told me that my son was going to have an unbelievable summer. I took the comment as a hidden message. She was not able to tell me what exactly would make it so unbelievable, so of course my imagination ran wild. Since he was said to be a good athlete (Brett and Kip both were exceptional athletes) and his summer was going to be incredible, my imagination leaped to a wild conclusion. He had to be participating in the Olympics. That meant he would be on the West Coast this summer.

I knew his name now, so I didn't go completely crazy watching as I had that winter. The announcers spoke of Greg Louganis being adopted. I wondered if his mother knew she was watching her own son win all those medals. ABC had done a beautiful story about the adopted brother and sister who skated together in the Winter Games, showing a home movie of the little backyard rink their adoptive parents had made for them. I had not known my son's name then, so any child who had been adopted might have been mine. I remembered thinking at the time how much those two kids were a product of both sets of parents. The adoptive parents had not seemed particularly athletic but they had lovingly sacrificed to build the rink. The children might have gotten their athletic ability from their biological families. When brother and sister skated, did they wonder if their birth families were watching? Did they want them to know, too?

The mind of a mother who does not know how her child is faring, is always roaming, always wondering about even remote possibilities. Aren't the children wondering and fantasizing, too? Couldn't knowing the truth be in everyone's interest?

Chapter Fifteen

B y the fall I had given up hope of hearing from my son or his mother through Soundex. If they were going to get in touch with me, they would have by now. He was probably in college. That would be a big enough adjustment for him without adding the disruption of my reappearance. My plan was to continue the search, so at least I could get hold of him in an emergency, and pray for the grace of patience that everyone seemed to advise me to ask God for. I was still not totally convinced waiting would be His first choice.

To help with the waiting, I joined a Bay Area group called PACER (the Post Adoption Center for Education and Research). It provided monthly workshops, seminars, and consultations for birth parents, adoptive parents, and adoptees. The first meeting I went to was in the home of an adopted woman in her early thirties. Julie had just met her birth mother, who would be at the meeting, too, as well as other newly reunited parents and grown children. It was almost dark when I found the house. I could hear the voices of little children as I approached. One of them opened the front door. I introduced myself to Julie and she introduced me to her mother, who was sitting a little bit apart from the group conversing inside. She looked like a sweet grandmother, which in fact she was. Most people think of unwed mothers as the teenagers they once were. Here was one with gray hair who had just met her daughter again after thirty years.

It felt a little uncomfortable walking into a room full of strangers, but I had often felt estranged, even among people I knew well. It went with the territory.

A small group was gathered around an attractive woman in her early fifties and a man who looked so much like her, he could only be her son. Both were articulate about their feelings for each other and their reunion. I was mesmerized as I listened to him say that he didn't know how he felt about his birth mother whom he had searched for and found.

"Is she my mother, my friend, like a lover, or an acquaintance? I feel a real strong and instant bond, a spiritual, mystical connection with her. But my adoptive mom is who I consider to be my 'real' mother. However, I always wondered about my first mother. When I was five and six years old, I would sometimes stick my head out the car window while driving with my family just in case she might pass by and recognize me."

His birth mother, Nancy, said, "I was eighteen when I became pregnant. When my mother learned of my pregnancy, she gave me a one-way ticket to Chicago. After I arrived in Chicago, I called a number of homes and was told there were no beds left. I felt strangely reassured, realizing I wasn't the only one. I was given an anesthetic and put out for the delivery. The last thing I remembered was that the gurney hit the double doors, and I called out 'Mama.' I never called my mother

'Mama.' The doctor advised me not to see the baby. He said it would be easier to forget. You never forget." Pain flickered across her face. "They are doing studies now that liken the experience to the post-traumatic stress syndrome experienced by Vietnam vets. You may go numb a dozen years after giving the baby up, then suddenly be overwhelmed with grief again. I deadened the pain and flashbacks and nightmares with alcohol."

When they met, her son seemed so familiar to her. "I had raised five boys and he blended so comfortably with them that I sometimes forgot I hadn't parented him." She paused. "None of my sons could ever replace my firstborn. They couldn't replace each other either. Each child has his own individual soul and is irreplaceable."

She surprised me by saying that she would never have searched. She did not feel she had the right to. At this point in the adoption rights movement, only 5 percent of birth mothers searched, she said.

When the meeting began, we went around the circle with brief introductions. Then the floor was open for discussion.

Nancy's son, Carlos, formally introduced himself as a family therapist and explained his involvement with PACER. Carlos described his search: "I felt a sense of destiny and mystery throughout my three years of searching. Looking back, I could see it could have been condensed into three weeks. But each little bit of information was almost too rich for me. Each piece of my identity had to be digested a little at a time as I began to feel rooted in the real world for the first time."

He and his birth mother met at the Holiday Inn in Chicago. "When I looked up from the newspaper I had been casually pretending to read, I saw a tall blonde woman approach the front desk with the exact same slouch I have. I could feel that slouch. I jumped up and walked towards her. Suddenly, I was not nervous at all, just relieved and pleased.

"My name is followed by the Roman numeral three. The family name comes from a man who arrived on the *Mayflower*. Being the third means I am supposed to be like them, and I'm not. I remember learning to write my name and being unable to finish it without knowing deep inside that I was hoaxing everyone. The only thing I really knew about myself was that I was a good artist, and no one in my adoptive family was an artist. About the time I was seven or eight, I remember thinking, I am who I am because I decide who I am. I am a talented artist because I paint all the time. What I have traced in a lot of adopted people is that they develop an existential anxiety about who they are and what is reality. When you are part of your biological family, it's easy to assume a lot of things. When you are adopted, you wonder. This is why adolescence can be particularly difficult. When I saw my birth mother and 'felt' her slouch and knew it as my own, I no longer thought of myself as a 'blank slate.' I found my brothers who were artists, too. Now, comes the task of integrating all of this.

"It's important to realize you are getting something positive from the search, no matter what the results," Carlos said. "Our relationship will change and grow for the rest of our lives."

Cathie introduced herself. She was thirty-four years old and adopted. She had enormous green eyes and a strikingly pretty face. I wondered what those eyes must have looked like in a baby's face and thought it was a tragedy that her mother never got to see her child grow up to become such a beautiful, sensitive woman. Her mother didn't even know she was a grandmother. Cathie said she decided to search after her child was born.

"I thought my son, Nicholas, would provide the vital blood

connection I had been missing. But he hasn't, and I am surprised that he couldn't. That's why I must search. I feel a deep, deep longing for that connection. I wonder if, at a profound level, adoptees feel disconnected from the Earth, like we are alien beings almost, just dropped here, but not a part of the planet by not being connected to the body that gave birth to us."

Morgan had searched for her daughter for eight years. She explained the need to know as the same panic any mother experiences when her child is lost, out of sight, for even a few seconds.

"Only this same powerful panic stays with *us* for all the years we are out of touch with our children. Women are not made to be able to give up their babies. The maternal instinct is too strong. How could it be otherwise?"

Marilyn, seated next to me, began to weep. Huge tears flowed down her cheeks. Her adopted son, Josh, was not yet three. She had mixed emotions about the adoption and how it was all handled. And she felt obsessed, at times, with Josh's birth mother. She felt enormous guilt at having so much happiness at what had to be a huge cost to her. She said it was difficult to hear all the birth mothers' and adoptees' stories. The last thing she wanted was unhappiness for Josh or his birth mother. Her tears kept flowing. Her story was pretty typical for an adopting mother.

"My husband and I had gone through all the testing available at the time. The tests subjected us to untold humiliation, including having to make love within an hour of particular office visits and then being examined. It was almost kinky. When it was confirmed that we were unable to conceive, we took a while to discuss options and decided adopting a baby would be best for us. We went to a lawyer who specialized in open adoptions. Unfortunately, the lawyer was more concerned with obtaining his fee than giving us knowledgeable guidance through the emotionally volatile process. We were advised how to 'package' ourselves, which was nothing more than further humiliation after the already degrading process of infertility testing. Not much later, the lawyer called with news that there was a woman interested in meeting us.

"Josh's mother came to our house when she was eight months pregnant. I cleaned for three days beforehand. She made the decision right there in the living room. I felt euphoric. I've never had that same feeling again. I'm a nice Jewish girl but I felt like the Virgin Mary. I felt beautiful and wonderful; for a whole year I had felt defective. When my husband and I made love that night, I felt we were making Josh.

"No one seemed to take into account our need to bond with the baby. The hospital called to notify us when labor began. I flew over to the hospital, only to be told that I could not see the baby. A nurse, seeing my frustration, allowed me to hold and care for a little girl baby. So, I accidentally bonded with that baby instead, and wanted to take her home with me. She was dark with big eyes and looked so much like me. Josh was fair, apparently taking after his father, not his mother, who looked a lot like me.

"When I brought Josh home, I wanted so much to establish a vital bond with him. I remembered in Greek mythology, upon adopting Herakles, Hera, wife of Zeus and protector of women in marriage and childbirth, clasped him to her breast and pushed him down through her toga, letting him drop from her as if she were birthing him. I tried that. I tried to nurse him, to give him something from my body that would nourish him and bond us. It didn't work. It's actually quite rare to produce milk. I just wanted to give him what he was missing from not being with his birth mother."

227

I found her story profoundly moving. It was so courageous of her to get right down to the raw feelings. The women who had given up their children poured out all kinds of reassurance to her, wanting so much for Marilyn to believe she had a right to her son.

She had broken down almost everyone's defenses. As Marilyn's tears subsided, another woman who said she was an adoptive mother spoke up. She and her daughter had launched the search for her child's birth mother together. The search took only a week. Now her daughter was feeling as high as a kite, but she felt horribly rejected.

When she said this, everyone in the group reacted as if a bucket of cold water had been thrown at them. We all fell back in our seats. This seemed to block any further discussion. This woman had struck us each at our core. We had been talking of joyful reunions. Was it inevitable that someone had to lose if the others gained?

I saw how common my story was. For some reason I had to hear over and over what had happened to other unwed mothers in the homes to believe it had really happened to me.

There are at least two million adopted children in the United States. The figures vary since data are hard to come by, because of the secrecy that has enshrouded adoption for so long. Probably this is an underestimate. Each of these two million children has adoptive parents, and often many more relatives, who are concerned for that child and love that child. This adds up to a lot of people. But there is another group no one enumerates, which is just as large. It is evident, once you think about it, that for every adopted child there is, somewhere, another mother, another father, and other relations—grandparents, aunts, uncles, cousins, brothers and sisters. The laws that make it difficult for a birth mother to search for her child, or for an adopted child to search for his or her birth mother and father, do a disservice to these people, too.

Wouldn't it be easier, and better, to face up to reality and acknowledge our existence, to permit adopted children to locate their birth parents, if they want to, and to permit birth parents to locate and seek a reconciliation with their biological children? Wouldn't this be the most generous, sane, and safe course?

Whether they meet or not, the other mother exists. Despite all efforts to suppress or deny this.

―――――

Early in November, I interviewed Carlos and his mother for an article to run in a local paper. It was a way for me to prepare myself. For the same reason, I found myself scrutinizing all nineteen-year-old males. It could have been embarrassing but I wanted to get an idea about what a young man that age was like.

Writing the article, however, made me depressed. Their story was so similar to mine that yet again I found myself reliving the past as if it were happening for the first time. In the middle of it, Chris called. He said he had been thinking about me strongly the past three days and wondered if I was okay. I felt comforted; I had felt very much alone, the same aloneness as I had endured at nineteen. We wondered if our son had inherited our telepathic abilities.

I asked Chris how his wife was handling all this. I felt she had to be a saint to be so accepting of this situation. He said she was an exceptional person, and they had always known this would happen some day. I wondered whether I would be so good, if I were in her position.

I phoned Emma Vilardi, founder of the Soundex Reunion Registry, to get some information for my article. She asked me about my own story. When I mentioned Chris's supportive involvement in the search, she said they had begun to hear in unprecedented numbers from fathers of children who had been relinquished. These men, she said, hoped for the chance to be reunited with their children. They were surprised themselves at their lasting feelings of guilt after their children were given up. They confided to her about their guilt at allowing themselves to be manipulated by their parents, or at having been too immature to do what was "right."

Then she said something that astonished me. My son and his parents might not realize they had enough information so that we could be matched in the registry. All these months I had believed they had deliberately chosen not to register, decided not to meet me. They might have wanted to but not realized they could succeed if they only knew what the birth certificate showed and the agency's name.

I intensified my search. I called information to get the listings of all the John Aloysius Ryans in the area of New York listed on my son's birth certificate. The neighborhood was heavily Irish and his surname was quite common. I also noted everyone with the maiden name of my son's adoptive mother. But I decided to start with the father. I dialed the first number and a woman answered. I said I was looking for a certain John Aloysius Ryan who would have been thirty-one in 1966.

"Yes," she said.

"And was he in the Marine Corps?"

"Yes."

"Well," I said, "I think we are talking about the same man. Did this man have an adopted son?"

It sounded like the phone had gone dead. Then, after a long silence, she said, "Well, actually, I wouldn't put anything past him at this point."

As it turned out, they had been separated for five years. He was *not* the same John Ryan, and I apologized profusely, feeling mortified.

Rather than risk another experience like that, I formulated a new tactic. It was the middle of December. I made another trip to the Sutro Library to get a list of Catholic churches in their town, hoping to find the one they had been married in or the one where my son had been baptized. Knowing I was so close now, I was afraid of making a false move and fretted about what story to tell to get the church to release the information. Finally, I decided to say I was an old friend of his mother's, had been in her wedding party. But we had lost track of each other over the years. I wrote the script out, knowing how nervous I would be about lying. Even after deciding on my story, it took me another whole day to screw up my courage to make the call. I was terrified that it wouldn't work.

First thing in the morning I called. A woman, a volunteer in the church, answered. I hoped she would be naive enough to go straight to the records and give me my son's address and phone number. Instead, she took down all the information, then told me she would have the priest get back to me. It might take a couple of days. I was downcast.

I had to leave the house to go grocery shopping. The cupboard was beyond bare. Going after three o'clock, when it would be after six back east, I felt safe. The odds of anyone calling that late were slim.

When I returned, just as I tried to open the kitchen door with bags of groceries in each arm, the phone rang. I got to it just in time. It was someone playing a joke, I thought. Then it became clear that this was the priest. He was Filipino, his accent so thick and his English so poor that we could not understand each other at all. We literally had to spell out our conversation.

He did confirm that my son's adoptive parents had been married in his church, but there was no record of a baptismal certificate. I spelled out, "Thank you very much for trying," and hung up. Now I had one last resort—one I had put off trying, afraid that it, too, might fail, leaving me hopeless. I resolved to hire a private detective to canvass all the states for my son's driver's license application. Grace was able to recommend a man to me, a friend of hers.

The detective's southern drawl was comforting. He told me when he did a search, he would go state-by-state alphabetically. I told him he didn't have to bother, he could just check out the Southern states, then New York, and then the Eastern seaboard. That was where I was sure he would find my son.

He promised that he would have his work completed by the Sunday after Christmas. That was only twelve days!

Two days before Christmas I wrote a pessimistic letter to Chris, telling him what I had done and how terrified I was that this would not work. Just after I mailed it, the phone rang. It was Grace. My heart started pounding like crazy.

"Carol, I wanted to be the first to tell you. The detective has found your son! And you will never guess! He found him in the forty-eighth state he tried!"

"What does that mean?"

"Didn't you ask him to start on the East Coast and go all the way west? He finally found your son in *California*!!"

I let out a scream. As I paced the kitchen floor, waiting for the investigator to call me with more information, I felt as if I were weightless. Where were Brett and Kip? It was dark out. I didn't have a clue what to cook for dinner. The phone rang. My heart stopped.

It was someone asking for help at a school function. I said I had to get off the telephone, to free my line for an important call, the most important one of my life. Unbelievably, she insisted on keeping me on the phone. I said, "Sorry," and hung up.

I put soup on for dinner. The phone rang again. It was the detective.

He sounded just as excited as I was. I apologized for making him work so hard when he would have gotten results almost right away, following his method of going state-by-state alphabetically.

He didn't care. He just couldn't believe we were *both* in California. The town in which my son was living was called Mission Viejo. It had a vaguely familiar ring to it, but I couldn't place it. He said my son was six feet tall, had brown hair and hazel eyes. I was getting goose bumps all over. But the family's telephone number seemed to be unlisted.

Of course. It would be! I thanked him profusely for being my Christmas angel. As soon as I hung up, I ran to get the atlas and looked up Mission Viejo. It was south of Los Angeles, just north of San Diego.

Oh, my God. I stared at the atlas, astonished. A gold star just north of San Diego . . . The clairvoyant.

I read on, trying to get a picture of what my son's home was like. "Mission Viejo was the first planned community in California." I remembered reading about it now. Their manmade lake was being filled by our water during our drought. Everyone in the north of California had been up in arms about it. I stared at the map for the longest time. My elation was indescribable.

Brett and Kip came home and I told them. They were excited, too. I had to explain that we couldn't get in a car and go down there right away. I had to tell myself that, too.

In my excitement, I made a million phone calls. Morgan, my PACER friend, was going to Los Angeles for Christmas. She promised to look up the address in a Polk Directory while she was there to get the phone number for me. She would call me as soon as she had it.

Christmas Eve and Christmas Day almost passed me by. On the twenty-sixth, Morgan called with the telephone number. But the listing was under a different last name.

Was there some mistake? Did I have the wrong address after all? I couldn't keep still, I couldn't stand the agony much longer.

After dinner, as soon as Brett and Kip were involved with a TV show, I poured myself a glass of wine and sat down in my favorite spot at the dining room table. The phone and the number, which I prayed was my son's, were in front of me. I wrote out a "script," so I wouldn't forget what I wanted to say. I felt almost light-headed. I took a sip of wine, dialed three of the numbers, and put the receiver back. I took another sip of wine. Dialed again and hung up. After repeating this several times, I decided it would be best if I waited. I could not do it yet. The kids were going to take the ferry into the city to see Ron on Friday morning. I would call then.

The whole next day I debated whether to ask for my son first or for his parents. It was between the two of us, really, I reasoned. I ought to talk with him first and leave the options to him. He'd had no say in decisions made when he was born. Now he should be in control of the things that affected his life. Yet it

234

was such a major event for him, I wondered if, as his parents, they *should* know first.

I respected them and I wanted no hard feelings. The last thing I wanted was for him to be put in the middle, which I had come to understand was a quite common result. My decision was to try to speak with him first, if possible. But after waiting nineteen years—half my life—all that mattered to me was that I speak to him and he to me, at long last.

Friday morning I sat in the car in front of the ferry terminal and watched the kids buy their tickets and go through the gate. The air was crisp and crystal clear and the sun was warm for late December.

Back home, I took a long shower and washed my hair. I put my makeup on extra carefully. I had always wanted to stay youthful. Both my parents were wonderful examples of individuals staying vibrant while getting older. Yet my desire to remain youthful seemed a little different. I had always hoped to stay as close as I could to who I was when I was last with my son.

As I got dressed, I began to feel I was getting ready for a job interview. Should I wear stockings? I wouldn't feel like myself in stockings, so I threw on a pair of clean jeans and the bright coral angora sweater I had bought in Rome.

Was she the type who was meticulously dressed even at breakfast? Was her house always immaculate? Did she bounce out of bed with perfect hair? She was certain to be a great cook. (Brett and Kip thought they had drawn the short straw when it came to choosing a mother who was a terrible cook.)

I grabbed one of the many pieces of paper I had written the telephone number on and walked down the stairs. It was about eleven o'clock. I made myself some coffee, found some paper and a pen, and sat down in the dining room. Sunshine was flooding through the French windows. I checked over my script and dialed once and hung up before it began ringing. This was ridiculous. I was shaking like a leaf. I kept putting off the crucial moment.

I called my friend Yvonne. "What if they don't want me in their lives? What if this is a horrible mistake? What if they hang up on me? Do I have a right to make this call?"

Yvonne had heard these fears many times by now. I had repeated them like a litany over the years. My friends had put up with a lot of my tedious self-doubt. She told me over and over that everything was going to work out fine. This was meant to be or I wouldn't have come this far.

I tried to get myself really, really calmed down. As soon as I could get all my thoughts off of myself and what might or might not happen, I could take action. I remembered again why I believed my son needed me to make this call—that there were things he needed to know about himself that only I could tell him.

I dialed.

The phone rang four times. And then a *little* voice answered. I asked, "Is John there?"

The little voice said, "No. He's in Kansas City learning to be an airline pilot."

My heart was pounding furiously. I had always imagined him in college.

"Is your mother home?" I asked.

"Just a minute. I'll get her." The little voice trailed off.

Half a minute passed. A woman's voice said, "Hello."

I went blank. I realized I had not written a script for talking to his mother. The last names were different; *this* John was in Kansas City. Maybe I had the wrong number again. This might not be the right family after all. I stared down at the paper, willing words to come to me. Then suddenly I found them.

"Is this Rosemary?" If her name was Rosemary, then she was my son's mother.

There was a little questioning pause. "Yes, this is Rosemary."

Everything began to swim in front of my eyes. "I have reason to believe . . . that I am your son's mother."

"Oh, wow," she said. "You have probably called at the right time. I am in a weakened state. I've been in bed with the flu for the past four days and Don, my husband, is in Kansas City for extra pilot training. Jack took one of his little brothers down to see their grandmother, so that I can have a little rest. He won't be back for a couple of hours."

They called him Jack. Jack.

"We never did get around to sending the form to that registry that the social worker told us about. Time has a way of getting by so fast. And Jack had such a busy summer. He lifeguards at the lake here at Mission Viejo, so it was good to have the information about any predisposition to skin cancer. After I heard about it, I took him to the doctor right away for a checkup. Sometimes I would wake up in the middle of the night and wonder if you were dying of cancer."

I felt awful that this was what my son had to do after first learning about me, that this was his first information about me. I wondered if it had given him a creepy feeling.

"He also went to China with the water polo team this summer. He's a terrific water polo player. He plays the hole position."

I had never seen a water polo match.

"It was funny. When Jack was growing up, we exposed him to everything, not knowing much about you or what to expect from him. At first, I didn't get him into any organized sports.

But then, when he got on the team, he would be voted 'most improved player' because his talent would come out." I told her that most of the people in my family had athletic ability.

"We used to pray for you every night," Rosemary said. "I always told Jack that you loved him when you gave him up. I just imagined what it would have been like for me in your situation.... I often wished I could have told you about different things he did."

I had been prepared, by what I had heard about adoptive parents, to expect far less of a greeting. I was moved—awed—by the generosity of her spontaneous response. This was what I believed should be possible between two women who share the same child, but I knew how lucky I was.

I thought I heard what was a sort of sigh and deep breath as she made the decision to let me into their life.

"Are you sitting?" she said.

"Yes."

"Before I tell you this, I want you to know that Jack is all right. He has had no problems and he is completely normal in every way."

I felt nauseous, suddenly.

"We did not get Jack until he was eight months old."

I swallowed hard. Salty tears instantly burned my eyes. Oh, my little baby. What had happened to you? I had always *known* something was wrong.

Rosemary said Jack had been placed with another couple first. And he had spent six weeks in a foster home before that couple got him. I asked if she was sure. That was the one thing I had demanded of Sister Dominic, that he go to his adoptive family right away.

She was sure, she said. The first couple that had been given my baby was young. The fellow was twenty-one, Chris's age.

And she was twenty, only a year older than me. Neither one had gone to college. Their marriage was shaky. A baby was supposed to keep them together. (*This* was the perfect couple, superior to Chris and me in every way, who would give my son far more than we could! How had they been approved for adoption?)

I asked what had happened. Rosemary assured me that Jack had not been abused. As soon as she got him, she had taken him to a doctor to have him checked to make sure.

I wanted her to keep going, and feared I wouldn't hear the whole story if she knew how much it was upsetting me.

They had called him Dennis. They had lived in Charlotte . . . I didn't know how much more I could listen to. He had been only twenty-five miles away when I was in college. He should have been in my arms.

When her husband walked out on her, the woman tried to raise him alone. The husband would come back when a social worker was scheduled to visit to make them think the marriage was all right. But then he changed his mind and informed on her. So the agency took the baby back.

Rosemary kept telling me over and over that Jack was fine. There were no repercussions. He was healthy and normal. But I was beginning to feel a terrible rage. My baby had had three names by the time he was eight months old!

I remembered—Chris and I were in the car, jasmine floating through the window, fearing for our baby, thinking our shared premonition meant we were unbalanced. There *had* been something wrong and somehow Chris and I had known it. We had wanted our baby back so much. If we could have gotten him, we would have said yes in a second and gotten married. That's all we wanted. When they needed a new family for our baby, Catholic Social Services could have called us first to ask if our situation had changed, if we had changed our minds. We were probably not considered at all when our baby needed another home. If they had only called to check!

Would they have put him in an orphanage rather than let us know where he was? Were we less qualified than an orphanage? I wondered what they would have actually done had we called to find out about him. Would they have lied and said he was fine and happy? Probably.

After he was returned by that set of adoptive parents, my baby had been put in *another* foster home, Rosemary told me. Those people fell in love with him and wanted to adopt him, but it was against regulations. When Rosemary and her husband (whom Jack was named after), got the call about an available baby, they had only one day to prepare. They had never expected an eight-month-old. The nuns had his hair cut real short. He looked like he had never been out in the sun. Rosemary couldn't wait to get him out in the fresh air. I was grateful.

As she told it, I could see it all. She and her husband put him in a car seat in the back of their Volkswagen Beetle, and Rosemary began to give Jack some food. She said he wouldn't swallow it. He gave her a look like he was going to spray it out all over everyone. Who could blame him? It seemed a good sign that he still had so much spirit left in him. Rosemary said she gave him back a look like, "Don't you dare!" He swallowed his mouthful and was a perfect baby from then on. Of course. He was a survivor.

They took him to their home in Camp Lejeune, North Carolina. He had been so close to Chris at college then. She said when Jack was given to them, she felt a great responsibility to me for all the trust I had put in the nuns to find him parents that would love him and take care of the him the way I would have wished to.

"God works through people," she went on. "And for some reason, He wanted Jack to be with me. Jack was my gift from God. You and Chris were His instruments." I kept quiet. "My husband John was killed in Vietnam when Jack was twenty-two months old. God must have known how much I would need Jack then. And if he had come to us as a tiny baby, John wouldn't have had the same joy in relating to him for the short time that was all we had together."

I wanted to change my position, but I was too weak. Tears streamed down my face. I felt very cold.

After her husband's death in October of 1967, she'd taken Jack with her to New York to live near her family in Queens. I had moved to New York City in November of 1968.

The adoption had not been finalized at the time of her husband's death. Rosemary said she had been terrified at the thought that I might have gotten married by then and, finding out that she didn't have a husband, would ask for my baby back.

"Would you have? Jack was often my only reason for living back then. I couldn't have borne losing him."

I didn't know what to say.

In 1971 she remarried, and they all moved to California. That was the same year Ron and I moved to California. They had lived in the East Bay, forty-five minutes from us. Ron had good friends who lived in the same town they did, and we often went to visit them. In fact, Ron had wanted us to move there.

For a brief time they had lived in Virginia, when Jack was nine. I told her Chris was from Virginia Beach. She said their next-door neighbors in Virginia had a home in Virginia Beach. They had a daughter who had been Jack's best friend during that time. She asked me to ask Chris if he knew their former neighbors. (It turned out, he did know them, and Jack's friend had also been good friends with Chris and Emily's son, Steven.)

They moved back again to the East Bay. At thirty-nine, she discovered she was pregnant for the first time. It had never occurred to her; she was sure she had cancer. Her son was born when Jack was ten. Afterward, she said she cried for me, realizing what I must have gone through giving Jack up. Then another son was born a year and a half later.

She said that once, when Jack was very little, he came up to her and, out of the blue, asked, "Who borned me?" I was grateful to her for having the courage to share that with me. "Jack and I were like clones, our personalities meshed so well," she said.

I wouldn't have wanted it any other way for them, but I felt a huge pang of jealousy.

We talked for four of the fastest hours I had ever spent. She said she hoped we would meet, that she felt she had a good friend in me, that we had a friendship that had lasted nineteen years. That was how *I* felt. What stronger bond could two women have, if we could find the courage to set aside our fears! I promised to send pictures and she promised to send pictures. I asked her not to pressure Jack into calling me, if he was too uncomfortable.

It was the hardest thing to hang up the phone and cut the connection. But we had to. My ear was literally in great pain. And I was in shock. It was late afternoon. I was freezing. No matter how many layers of clothes I put on, I couldn't get warm.

He had been well loved and taken care of. Knowing this was a tremendous relief. Yet hearing about my own son's life from a stranger—even a wonderful one—was painful.

I had not been there. He did not know my touch, my look. I had missed all of his growing up. I missed being loved by him. I was, after all, a total stranger to him. He would never know me that way. But he was okay and had been well loved. I was grateful to her.

Chapter Sixteen

I gathered the pictures I wanted Jack to have. Knowing now
that he had none of himself for the first eight months of his
life, I included a lot of baby pictures of Brett and Kip, in case he
might have looked like either one of them as an infant. I also
included pictures of my family; perhaps he resembled one of
them. My sister Janice had sent me a picture of Chris and me
before my senior prom, and I included that, although I felt
embarrassed by my resemblance to Alice in Wonderland in the
photo. I also included a few baby pictures of myself and some
views of the various houses we had lived in. Which pictures
would he respond to?

I tried to imagine what it would be like for Jack to finally see
people he was related to, people he might look like. Had he, like
Cathie, yearned to reconnect to something he did not understand but knew he needed? Had he felt lost at the core of his
being? Could any amount of love make up for that loss?

It frightened me to pose these questions. I feared the answers.
I didn't want him to have suffered. But I didn't want to keep

pretty pictures in my head either just so I would not have to worry. Then I wouldn't be able to help him, should he need my help.

Cathie, who had loved her adoptive family, had still felt a dissonance in her body. Her body had always registered a difference: different smells, hair texture, touch. She believed that in some way she had been disconnected on a primal level from nature. But perhaps women felt that more than men.

I knew an adopted woman who had written her doctoral dissertation on the comparison between patients diagnosed as "borderline personalities" who were adopted and those raised with their original families. "Borderline personality" patients are loosely described as having two personalities, one presented to others and one based on interior fantasy. Apparently, adopted people were often misdiagnosed as having "borderline person-alities" when in fact their so-called fantasy self was close to the truth of who they actually were. Adopted children were often better off when there was a huge discrepancy in physical appearance between them and the parents with whom they had been placed. When there was a great similarity and everyone could pretend the child truly came from the adopted family, then there was no permission for the child to be the person he felt himself to be. This created feelings of great psychic isolation and made genuine intimacy in social relations difficult.

From my conversation with Rosemary, Jack had not been affected as profoundly as some.

I sent the package on New Year's Eve and included a letter from Chris and one from myself, plus a copy of *The Adoption Triangle: The Effects of the Sealed Record on Adoptees, Birth Parents and Adoptive Parents,* by Dr. Arthur D. Sorosky, Reuben Pannor, and Annette Baran. I hoped this book would help them as it had helped me. This was a risky situation for all of us. I told myself over and over that I was capable of waiting, that I would not buckle under the strain.

Some friends had little sympathy for what I was feeling. Someone volunteered I had a selfish need to ruin my son's life. I even received an anonymous letter, attacking me for attempting to contact my son. His parents were the ones who had raised him and they were the only ones he needed, it said. I was only interfering. I had signed the papers. I needed to take responsibility for my decisions. Being a mother to Kip and Brett should be enough for me.

I wondered who could be so threatened by what I was doing as to write such a letter. To my mind, my need to search for their half-brother could only indicate to Brett and Kip how powerfully I did love them. If either of them had been Jack, I would have done no less.

On the second of January, Brett and Kip and I went skiing. We came back on the fifth. I hoped to find a letter and pictures awaiting us, too. But there was nothing. Each time the telephone rang, it felt like an electric shock. But it was never Jack. Waiting was making me nuts. I began to feel again like I had felt at the home: I was the needy one; I really didn't deserve to ask for anything; they had all the power; I was at their mercy. Waiting made me remember feeling so vulnerable.

They had probably just gotten caught up in their normal lives and kept forgetting to mail the package of photos, I told myself. I made excuses, but I began to feel panicky. Jack would be nineteen on the ninth.

There was a PACER meeting on January 8 and I went. The fluorescent lights in the meeting room glanced off the aluminum chairs and tabletops. It was not a very comforting room, yet this was the one place where we could come and no one would think we were irrational. I desperately needed the help of the group about whether or not to call Jack on his birthday.

I told them about the wonderful conversation I had had with Rosemary, how I had felt so positive about it. Yet I had heard nothing. They had to have received my pictures at least four days ago and still there had been no response. And they had never registered with Soundex. Plainly there was a great deal of ambivalence towards me, even if it was unacknowledged. I told the group how much I wanted to call Jack on his birthday, but at this point, I felt the message was clear that they really were not ready to have me in their lives, even on the periphery. They might never be ready. What, I asked, did they think?

They responded loud and clear. "Call him!" I closed my eyes in a silent prayer. When I opened them, my eyes caught the eyes of Greg, twenty-six. He had been searching for his mother for two years. He looked straight at me and said, "Call him." (When Greg finally traced his mother three years later, he discovered she had died at about this time. He never got to meet her.)

———

I planned to call in the evening, since Jack had been born at night. This would give them a chance, if they were waiting for his exact birthday, to call me. I wanted to call at 6:51, adjusting Jack's birth time to the three-hour difference on the West Coast. No, they might be sitting down to dinner then. I waited. Finally I *had* to call.

Rosemary answered. Her voice sounded cool, as if she would prefer to hang up. I asked her if anything was wrong.

Some people had told her she had been foolish to be so open and accepting of me. They felt I had no right to come into her life. I knew enough to expect this. It was a very typical reaction, far more frequent than ready acceptance. I had heard it so many times in the past year, had consoled so many tears caused by it. But now, when I heard this reproach addressed to me, I felt unclean and frightened.

I told Rosemary this reaction was quite common. I felt in my heart that she didn't want to listen to their advice. I asked what she and Jack had thought of the pictures.

They loved seeing them. But they had not yet sent theirs.

When my package arrived, Rosemary said she had been dying to open it, but of course she waited for Jack to come home. Then, when he did get home, he waited three hours to unwrap it. She said he kept approaching it, then walking away. Finally, he opened it. His first reaction was that he really didn't think he looked like anybody. He was delighted to see he had worn the same tux to his senior prom as Chris had when he took me to mine. Jack had taken a girl with the last name of Schaefer to his prom. He ran upstairs and brought down an eight-by-ten black-and-white portrait of himself taken at about ten months and compared it with a black-and-white of me at six months. He began to see some resemblance.

Rosemary said she covered up the hair on a picture of me when I was pregnant with Brett and it was as if Jack was staring back at her. She couldn't get over it. She had always felt there had been a resemblance between Jack and herself, too, and some of his cousins looked just like Jack, she said.

We had talked for two hours. We were about to get off the phone, when Rosemary said, "I heard the door slam. Jack's home."

"Oh my God," I said. "Do you want me to hang up, so he has a chance to consider whether he wants to talk with me?"

And then he was on the phone, saying, "Hi!"

Love flooded my body but my mouth wouldn't work. I tried to squeak out a "hello" but literally could not form the word. Had I died? This was embarrassing. It felt like eternity. Then I could feel my feet touching the hardwood floor in the kitchen again. I said, "Hi," wishing I could explain why I had to be silent for another moment. Silently was how I had always loved him. It's how I knew him. The only sound I had ever heard him make was his first cry.

He said, "I knew it was you when I walked in the door and saw my mom on the phone."

"Did you want to talk? I didn't want to put you on the spot."

"Of course I did."

He wasn't angry. I couldn't believe it. I felt forgiven. Did I deserve to be? I said, "Your voice sounds so much like Chris's, but without his southern accent."

Anything I could think of to say seemed ridiculous compared with the significance of this moment. But I didn't want to overwhelm him. I talked about his reaction to the pictures. He thought it was great to have two more brothers. "I wrote them a letter," he said and won my heart for another eternity. He said he told them he hoped they didn't mind that he wasn't John Elway.

We talked about his water polo and he asked where he got his flat feet. This was funny. I couldn't imagine what it must have been like for him not to know these things. From my brother Bob, I told him. Bob's were flat as a pancake. Kip's are just as flat, too. How odd that my brother Bob, who had no children of his own, had passed his flat feet on to another generation. I told

Jack not to complain. They must have helped a great deal with his water polo. He told me about his trip to China. He said he was glad to see from the family photos that there was little chance he would go bald.

I asked him about his keeping Ryan as his last name. He said he had only decided when he went to get his driver's license. Up until then, he had used his stepfather's last name for school. I told him I was most grateful for his decision. I might never have found him if he had taken another last name.

We talked for half an hour. It was past midnight, and I was already exhausted after talking with Rosemary for two hours. I needed to get off the telephone so I could go outside and scream my joy to the heavens. I couldn't contain it in my body any longer. I had actually heard his voice, I had finally spoken with my son.

There was so much to say that I hadn't known where to begin. From his voice, I felt it was safe to believe I would be accepted, would become a part of his life. He promised to send the photos to me the next day. I made him swear he would. I told him waiting was horrible. He said he could understand.

I said goodbye and went outside. It was freezing and the stars were clear and sparkling, and closer than I could ever remember them. I was glad it was so cold. I needed the extremes of temperature to match what was going on inside me. Bodies are not equipped to feel so much joy. Mine felt like a fireworks display. Finally I cooled myself down and went upstairs to bed and fell into a deep sleep. All the next day, I found that no music was loud enough, the ocean not big enough, to counter my emotions. I practically had to tie myself to a tree to keep from hopping into the car and driving down to L.A. to see him, and Brett and Kip would have been right there with me.

I was so please to tell them how wonderful he sounded and

that he had written them a letter. All of this was a risk for everybody, but at least the rest of us were older. Brett and Kip were so young and vulnerable. I hoped that everything would go well for the sake of their wide-open hearts, as well as my own.

I figured I had two days of peace before I started my watch over the mailbox again. I filled the time calling my family and friends to let them know. Chris was thrilled. I promised to get copies made of the pictures for him as soon as I could. I told him I felt Jack would be very receptive to a call.

The third day the vigil started again. My mailbox yielded nothing, nor anything the next day. Little worries about how Rosemary—or any adoptive mother—would handle the situation began to surface in my mind. Had I gone too fast? Had I said too much, or alarmed her or Jack without knowing it? Nine days after talking with Jack the pictures still had not arrived.

On the tenth, I came home late in the afternoon. Taped on the front door was a notice from the mailman of an attempted delivery. Kip had been home at the time but he had not heard the doorbell. As calmly as I could, I asked him why he hadn't heard the mailman.

"Oh, it's probably just my bowling ball," he said.

I looked at him in disbelief. "You are expecting a *bowling* ball in the mail?"

"Yes. Dad ordered me one for Christmas."

I pitied the poor postal clerk if he handed me a package with a bowling ball instead of my son's pictures.

Anticipating the worst, I set off first thing in the morning for the post office. I was at the door just as they opened, offered the clerk my receipt, and held my breath. It wasn't the bowling ball. I gave him a long look of gratitude and cradled the package to my chest like a newborn baby. Back in my car, I sat behind the wheel and tried to will myself to wait until I got home. Impossible. I pushed the seat back as far as it would go.

Here was my son's own handwriting on the envelope. I imagined his hand when it was little, holding a big crayon and struggling to form letters, graduating from printing to cursive. And now he had a mature handwriting, beautiful and easy to read. The first time he had ever written my name. What did it feel like to him?

The first photo was his high school graduation picture. He looked a lot like me and just exactly how I had always imagined him: the build, the smile, the look in his eyes. He seemed so familiar. He had Chris's forehead. He was so handsome.

They had been extra generous; there were tons of pictures. They were in no order, so I saw him at around ten, then at one, then at sixteen. The absence of infant pictures seemed a crime. Then I came to a picture of Jack at about six and my heart stopped. There was Kip staring back at me. And then there was another one that was Kip again.

Jack seemed to have a build that was like Brett's, a certain way of standing and holding his head that seemed so much like Brett. At the same time, I could see why Rosemary said people never thought he was adopted. There were some pictures where they looked quite a lot alike. She was my height, fair and very attractive. In the pictures with his cousins, there was also an amazing resemblance. Rosemary had said they had all been so close. And there were a couple of photos of Jack as a toddler with her first husband. Jack had been named for him. It was obvious in the snapshots how crazy he was about Jack.

I read the letter Jack had written to me. It was very sweet, as was the one to Brett and Kip. He seemed pleased to know he came from a good family and said he had sometimes wondered who we were. He also said he loved his family and felt fortunate to have the mother he had. He said it was strange that we had lived so close to one another when they had the house in the East Bay. One of the pictures was taken on the Fourth of July in Sausalito, only a ten-minute drive from us. My mother had taken a picture of Brett and Kip and me on that exact same day, when she had been visiting. Ten minutes. . . .

One of the pictures I had sent was of me with two good friends, Marybeth and Lynne, at the Vic Braden tennis ranch, nine or ten minutes from his home. The coincidences were eerie.

With the joy came reality. There he was, his whole life in pictures, standing alongside people who were complete strangers to me, lovely-looking people sitting next to him, holding him in their arms, but strangers. My son was so familiar yet we had not met. I longed to hold my baby. But he was a grown man.

Brett and Kip would consider themselves far too old for hugs from their mother. It would probably frighten Jack, if he knew how much I needed to touch him. It frightened me. It was such a primal response. My body still needed to hold the child that it had not been allowed to nurture. My mind could not console my body. I longed to hold him with all my heart.

After journalism class, I walked back to my car. Just as I was getting into it, I spotted Brett and his friend, Mark, on their dirt bikes, cutting across the campus to get home from middle school. I waved them over. "Brett! I have the pictures." I showed him mostly the current ones, knowing he would be pretty bored

253

looking at the baby pictures. He was excited. When I showed him the one of Jack going to the prom with a gorgeous date, he asked if he could take that one to show his friends what his brother looked like. I said of course.

Through the rearview mirror, I watched Brett and Mark race back to school on their bikes. I watched them until they disappeared from view. I turned to start the car. Golden sunlight sparkled all through the deep green of the cypress trees. The moist shadows held the heavy fragrance captive. I opened the sun roof and felt grateful. I looked up at Mount Tamalpais. Only the peak was visible above the tree line. She was like an ancient mother goddess to our county. Her presence was comforting, a little pat on the head that said, "Patience. We have eternity." Most of the time, I only got the message subliminally. Now it came soaring into my heart.

My life was beginning to make sense again. I could not remember feeling so alive. I breathed in the miraculous air and looked through the pictures for the hundredth time. I felt almost whole.

Chapter Seventeen

Months passed. No formal invitation was extended to meet my son. I was tired of being obsessive, of waiting. The past year had been so intense. I wanted my life back. I wanted to be normal like everyone else, to be able to say, "I have three sons," without feeling guilty for saying it.

Taoists explain grace in a way different way from our idea of the concept. The Tao is the flow of the cosmos and most likened to the action of water as it fills up empty spaces, finds the places of least resistance and flows around obstacles, eventually wearing them down, pausing to fill deep places and then flowing on. The only way I could keep in the flow of my life was to love my son silently, let my love move quietly around all obstacles. It felt powerful to love that way. It came from inside me and no one was able to take away the love I kept to myself.

I needed time to assimilate all the great changes that were happening inside me, changing me, changing my relationships. I realized the terror I had felt for so long at the depths of my being, from not knowing about my child's welfare. I fully realized its power only when it was suddenly gone. Maybe that part of me that had stayed with Jack could come back to me now, because I knew he was safe. There was no longer a need to be detached from my feelings. My memory was returning as well. Whole chunks of my life came flooding back.

I could begin to enter fully into relationships again; I no longer needed to protect myself so fiercely. The feeling of being too different, that prevented true intimacy, was fading. I felt genuinely good about myself again, a part of the human race.

I could rearrange the furniture without feeling panicky. I could actually throw things out when I cleaned closets. I had not thrown out one thing in all those years. Even though I didn't have Jack, I had the brown corduroy maternity dress I had worn at Seton House. I had also kept the ski sweater with the one wrong stitch and the robe my parents had given me for my Christmas there. It was tattered, but I could not let it go. I had kept all of Brett and Kip's baby clothes, even the ones too stained to wear again. Irrational fear would rip right through me whenever it was necessary to throw something out. Because I had been directed to do the most impossible thing in the world for a conscious, caring woman, I had clung to things as compensation.

Brett and Kip were with Ron for the long Easter week end. Four days. A long time to be by myself. I felt at loose ends. The first day, while I was shopping for the kids, I wandered into a little bookstore called Paper Ships and bought a couple of books about reincarnation.

My old fascination with the subject was rekindled. The concepts led me way beyond anything I had ever imagined, into truths I felt I had always known. I took a long walk after reading. I needed to come back to planet Earth before the kids came home. Long walks were calming.

When I got back, I hid the Easter eggs, then went up to my room and found the tape of my session with John the clairvoyant. I popped the tape into the cassette deck, got comfortable, and listened.

"I get the word 'South.' Is he south of here?"

I listened to myself saying he was born in the South. But Jack actually had been south of *here*. John had also been right about the family not being southern conservative and that he hadn't been raised by narrow-minded people. He had been right that Jack had had good chances and a good upbringing. School had been very much on his mind, as he had been trying to get into USC on a water polo scholarship. I heard my surprised voice when I was told I would be the first to meet him, not Chris back in the East.

I heard John's voice saying, "I can't believe what I'm looking at because it looks like the Fresno/Bakersfield area. I kept thinking no. Yet, I can't get it to go somewhere else. There's a pull over there. Perhaps a few short trips. You also have a lot of affinity for the Los Angeles beach community, Long Beach, Redondo Beach. And I see a great big gold star just north of San Diego. When you go there, you'll be there with somebody or for somebody. A good relationship, but not a marriage or anything romantic. This looks like something developing over a period of time."

I clicked the tape off and sat very still. A shiver ran down my spine. This reading had been done six months before I found out where Jack was, two months before I knew his name.

The Yugoslavian painter in Paris had "seen" my son. The palm reader had "seen" the trauma it had been for me to give him up. I remembered trembling as I drove past Charlotte. Chris and I really had known something was very wrong with our son then. I hadn't been crazed.

Women separated from their children at birth whom I had met seemed to be extremely telepathic. Each time this concept was discussed within our support groups, it seemed to explain so much of what otherwise seemed unexplainable.

Sometimes, in my conversations with Jack, I felt we could communicate better telepathically, empathetically. It was an incredible situation, this talking with one's child who was so familiar, yet not.

Recently, during our longest phone conversation so far, Jack and I were comparing notes about how it had been for him, moving around so much. He told me the worst year of his life was the first year he had moved down to Mission Viejo. He had felt so alone that year—the year Ron and I separated, the same year both my mother and Chris had thought of wanting to search.

I had hoped that my prayer to the Blessed Mother, my last link to any spirituality, had worked and kept us connected. Rosemary had repeated almost the exact words of my prayer when we had talked. Had she heard it in the ether?

I seemed to be the one who initiated all the telephone calls and I worried that I was being a pest. Often Rosemary answered. We talked comfortably. She was such a generous, confident, compassionate person. But I feared that we had diverted the process from Jack.

She wrote me a beautiful letter, thanking me for finding him, explaining that she would feel sorry for a child whose mother did not search. In some ways, she felt it was best if the mother searched instead of the child, as proof of the mother's love for the child she had given up. It was so important, she felt, that the child know that the mother had never forgotten.

She was undoubtedly right, because when I asked Jack if I was being too pushy, he said he needed me to be the one to make all the contact in the beginning. He needed to be sure that I would not leave him, abandon him again, before he felt safe enough to emotionally reciprocate.

His comment gave me insight into some of the wild acting out I had heard of when some birth parents contacted the children they had relinquished. I had heard of cases where children stole or demanded things from their birth parents, some so angry that it was frightening to be around them. Maybe they had to test the strength of the bond or were expressing anger at being abandoned in the first place. The intensity of their pain seemed, in a convoluted way, to validate the depth of the loss, and thus the power of the bond.

———

Chris felt reluctant to push himself on Jack, but I always encouraged them to get to know each other. They obviously resembled one another in possessing great patience. After five months, Jack called Chris. They talked for three hours.

By mid-May, I was getting very anxious. We still had made no plans to meet. Then Brett and Kip signed up for a football camp in late June down in Los Angeles. This was perfect. I didn't want them to feel left out. We could all meet Jack together. I called to tell Jack and Rosemary about our plans and we all agreed to meet at the end of June. I made reservations at an expensive hotel right on the beach, making certain that I had a room facing the ocean. We all had a month to prepare ourselves.

We left on Thursday, the twentieth of June, the day after my thirty-ninth birthday. I decided to drive down the Coast route, which takes twice as long. Why not throw in a little scenery and California history when you take your children on a trip to meet the brother they never knew?

Before I even turned on the ignition, my jaw was clenched tight. I was willing us to have fun. Brett built a tent in the backseat with sheets and pillows, put his Walkman on and tuned the whole thing out.

First came the scenic Seventeen-Mile Drive. The kids were getting carsick. That was not in my script. And then I insisted we had to take a jaunt through idyllic Carmel. They raced through the mission, barely taking note of anything. They said it felt creepy. Outside, I begged them to sit by a little fish pond so I could take a couple of pictures. Brett broke off a branch from a nearby bush and posed, pretending to be fishing. Then they tore around, chasing each other, completely disturbing the tranquillity of the mission. I followed them, penitently eyeing the disapproving tourists. I was already strained to the limit and we had barely begun our journey.

But I was determined to make this a memorable family trip. Next stop, lunch at Nepenthes in Big Sur, atop a cliff overlooking the ocean. The view was spectacular. They would have preferred McDonald's. Actually, they would rather have flown down to L.A. I could only hope my kids were getting something from this trip subliminally. We had at least nine more hours to go.

The road was narrow, cut into the side of the coastal mountains. At times there were sheer drops down to the surf. Brett emerged from under the tent now and then, when I especially insisted he look at a particularly beautiful sight. Kip sat peacefully next to me in the front seat, in some ways anchoring me. My hands got sweaty and slipped a couple of times on the steering wheel. Vivid flashbacks invaded my consciousness — the ambulance attendants wheeling me into the brightly lit emergency room as I was in labor with my first baby just as I rounded a sharp bend in the road, the woman screaming in the bed next to me. A wispy memory of patting my belly, feeling Jack rolling around in response, as I prepared the Seton House altar for Mass. The images kept coming unbidden.

"Are you suffocating yet, Brett?" I asked, and, as I glanced back over my shoulder to see his tent, I saw, instead, the curtain closing on the nursery window, and Jack's little head, with all the dark hair, disappearing. As the tires of the car rolled over pebbles, I heard the bassinets being wheeled down the hall. My heart leapt with joy remembering his eyes, that first look. And then I was holding him, saying goodbye, walking out of the hospital with Mrs. Hogan, freezing, with snow flurries all around me, my old prematernity dress unable to turn me back into who I used to be, my baby alone, left there.

As we moved inland toward San Simeon, I began to feel better. The jagged coast receded. Brett emerged from his tent. The late afternoon and early evening sun was soft and gentle and the road straight and wide over rolling hills. We reached San Simeon as the sun was setting and the sky was a rosy violet. I talked with the boys about seeing the famous Hearst Castle the next day. Complaints started right away. "We just want to get to the beach and meet Jack," they said practically in unison. "We don't care about that castle."

"You mean you want to drive some more tonight and get closer to L.A.?" I asked. That's what they wanted. So we found the motel at San Simeon, changed our reservations to another motel farther south, and hit the road, light-hearted for the first time since I'd planned the trip.

The following morning we set out again. We all loved the drive through Santa Barbara and got more and more excited as Los Angeles approached. I got lost for a little while around Redondo Beach, and then found my way to a freeway. We arrived at the Surf and Sand at Laguna Beach a little after two o'clock. The kids ran down to the water at once. There was only a narrow strip of beach between hotel and ocean. I could look straight down from the balcony and watch them.

I hoped they would want to meet us tonight. They knew we were arriving. We were separated by twenty minutes. It was incredible to contemplate.

I took a lot of time unpacking, getting my bearings after the drive, trying to feel comfortable and settled in the room. Every few moments, I would look out to the ocean for reassurance. I checked to see the boys were safe and, finally, sat on the edge of the bed facing the telephone on the nightstand. One last, quick glance at the ocean and I dialed. As usual, Rosemary answered.

I told her we had arrived and asked when we could get together. Would they like to come over for a swim and then go out to dinner?

No, Jack was working and she and her husband had just shampooed the carpet. The whole house was upside down. They had not planned to see us until the next day. Could we come first thing in the morning for breakfast? She gave me the directions and we said goodbye.

I stood out on the balcony and let the ocean soothe my frazzled nerves. This last period of waiting had to be gotten through. I thought to myself that of course she wanted to control the meeting by putting limitations on it. Understandably, she would want to protect her son from a total stranger, even if the stranger was his birth mother. (In fact, as I later learned, it was Jack who'd insisted everything be "perfect" before we arrived.)

I had heard many horror stories of adoptive parents changing phones to unlisted numbers, writing threatening letters through lawyers, turning the children against their birth mothers. So I was thankful for Rosemary's generosity. The harsh reality was that I had surrendered my child to adoption. The definition of "surrender" was to hand over power to another, to resign, to yield to emotion, to cease resistance. To give oneself up into the power of another; to capitulate.

To adopt was defined as receiving the child of another and treating him as one's own. Wishing things were different did me no good.

I went down to the beach and watched Brett and Kip. We ordered room service for dinner and watched television. I wanted to say something to my young sons to prepare them, but I didn't know where to begin. I kept hoping Jack might call on the spur of the moment and come over to meet us. It would be so much easier if our meeting were spontaneous. But he didn't. I took a picture of the setting sun to record the last day of not knowing my son.

Brett and Kip woke up early and, without my telling them, they dressed in their neatest clothes. They looked so handsome and I was so proud of them. The TV never even got turned on. I checked and rechecked, making sure I had the directions three times before setting out. They were complicated, so I had to concentrate on my driving. I made no mistakes and, suddenly, we were on his street.

And as soon as I realized it and looked up to find their house, there Jack was. He had just walked out the front door. He was picking up a tricycle to clear the path.

Jack looked down the slope of the front lawn and saw our car pull up. He smiled when he caught sight of us. He had a great smile — tender and sweet, shy and happy, and full of humor. He captured my eyes again just as he had when I held him as a baby. I was mesmerized. Like I had then, I felt I had known his soul for eons.

As he walked down the slope of the lawn to greet us, my knees buckled. I knew, looking straight at one another, that we had never been apart. In that instant, I *knew* it.

Car doors slammed as Brett and Kip piled out. The sound jarred. I felt a little confused and disoriented for a second. Rosemary and her two young sons, Mark and David, came out to greet us. I got out of the car. My whole body had turned to jelly and had no strength. I watched as Jack shook hands with Brett and Kip and told myself to get a grip. Thank God I wasn't crying. Jack and I gave each other an awkward, wonderful hug. I was acutely aware of everyone around us.

We turned toward the house, filed in the front door, through the living room and out to the back. I wanted to see Jack's room, walk through the whole house, take in his life there, but that would have been rude.

We all sat around a white table outside. Jack and Kip sat next to each other across from me. Kip was wonderful, so serious, sitting next to Jack. They were both the silent, observant type. Brett played catch with Mark and David on the lawn behind us. I was mute. Thank goodness Rosemary was a good talker.

Jack brought out his yearbook and showed off his school, his friends, the water polo team. Was I coming across as retarded as I felt? My mouth wouldn't work.

With so many impressions to absorb, it was nearly impossible to focus. I wanted to tell Jack what I was feeling. I caught him studying me and I felt he knew what it was like for me.

Then Jack's stepfather came out to join us. I had sensed he was resistant to this meeting, but I could see him realize now that we were simply regular folks like everybody else.

Rosemary wanted to take us down to the lake where Jack worked and show us all around and then have lunch. Her husband promised to join us afterward at the hotel for a swim.

We were all trying to be as normal as humanly possible, to make this a social meeting. But the feelings churning around threatened to become overwhelming. I felt I was walking a tightrope. If I showed any emotion at all, it would upset everyone and the day would end early. Rosemary confided that her sons, Mark and David, were a little afraid that we would take their big brother from them.

Rosemary seemed confident and in control and very sure about her relationship with Jack, just as Elinor had reported. Brett and Kip seemed fascinated with Jack, but I could see they didn't know what to think about it all either. I began to wonder if this was a one-time visit. Would we all satisfy our curiosity and then just go back to our normal, separate lives?

We drove through the streets, past his high school, and stopped by the recreation center. I saw the pool where he played water polo. His life was very different from what it might have been with Chris and me. Rosemary and her husband were very different from us. They were lovely people and she knew my son far better than I did, even though I sensed I knew him in a way she perhaps didn't. She noted things about him I would have never noticed, because they would have been second nature to me. Every once in a while, she would say, "Jack, hold your shoulders back." And I would straighten mine at the same time. My dad had always told us to keep our shoulders back. We did tend to slump our shoulders. As I observed Jack, I learned things about Brett and Kip, too. I had never noticed certain behaviors until I saw that they shared these with Jack.

After our tour, we went back to the house. Before we left for the beach, Jack's father showed me his orchard and I felt I got to know him a little better. As soon as they arrived at the hotel, all the boys raced into the water. Rosemary asked Jack to go down with them, as Mark and David were too young to be without supervision. I managed to take a picture from the balcony of Jack, Brett, and Kip together in the water.

Rosemary and her husband wanted us to walk around Laguna Beach while the kids swam. I wanted to just sit on the beach and watch Jack, but I thought it would be rude to refuse, and besides, I wanted to get to know them, too. And I wanted them to know me, so they would feel safe enough to let me into Jack's life. I was terrified now at the possibility of never seeing him again.

Jack had to leave to be at work at the Black Angus restaurant by four o'clock, so we went back to spend some time with him before he left. When we were alone, Rosemary began to ask questions about what it had been like at the home, giving up Jack. Jack came in and sat with us. He wanted to hear, too. I could feel that. But as I tried to tell them, I got all choked up and tears came, and I was afraid I was going to lose it. At that moment, with Jack in the room, realizing what I had done giving him up, I was about to faint.

This all had happened so very long ago. How could my feelings be so overpowering now? I apologized for being unable to tell them about it and promised that someday I would. I could tell that Jack didn't want to go, even as he let himself out.

Rosemary and I talked a little and then the others joined us. We wondered where we should all go for dinner. I couldn't imagine anywhere else but the Black Angus.

We met at the restaurant at seven o'clock. It wasn't until we were all seated in a big booth that I became aware of waiters and waitresses walking by, trying to catch a glimpse of me. Jack must have told them about me. I was thrilled that he wanted them to know. Jack came by to talk every chance he had. I got the feeling from his big smile that he was really pleased. I melted every time I saw him. He introduced the girl he was dating.

After dinner we went back to their house to see some home movies. Jack promised to come by right after he got off from work. (Each time I said goodbye to him I felt a wrenching pain, even though I knew I would see him again soon.)

The movies were great. Then Rosemary lined up Jack, Brett, Kip, and me to take pictures: left profiles, right profiles, full face, like a police lineup. She loved details and said it would be so much fun comparing noses and mouths and stuff. I was grateful for her powers of observation, because I learned so much about Jack's life from her. It was as if she hadn't forgotten anything.

It was one-thirty in the morning. We all had run out of steam. We were shocked it was that late. I said, "Let's get together again. I'll be here for a week." There was no response. Did they not hear me? Was this it? I walked slowly down the front lawn to the car to give them a chance to say, Okay, let's get together again! Maybe they wanted to think it over. But what if they thought it over and decided they didn't need to see us anymore? I hugged Jack and got into the car with Brett and Kip. I was shaking. The street was dark as I turned the car around. Theirs was the only house with the lights on on the block. I looked over my shoulder and watched Jack walking up the lawn to the front door where Rosemary was standing, still waving good bye. We waved back. It was impossible not to wish Jack could come back with us. I was terrified of not seeing him again.

From out of the darkness of the backseat, Kip said, "Mom, he seems so familiar to me."

"Me, too," I said.

The hotel room was dark when we opened the door. Through the huge windows, moonlight danced across the ocean waves. I flipped on the light and helped the boys pile into bed. We had to be up early to get to football camp in time. As I straightened up their clothes, I noticed a strange pair of sunglasses. They were Jack's. I guessed that at least a part of him did want to see us again.

We left early for the camp. During the drive back, I questioned whether I had the right to ask Rosemary if I could have a little time alone with Jack. I didn't know why I felt I had to ask her permission. He was nineteen. I had been nineteen when I gave him up. I doubted Rosemary would feel I needed to ask her permission, but I was psychologically back in the past. I knew it was ridiculous to feel so powerless and unworthy, but I did. Despite what I had done with the rest of my life, having been an unwed mother still made me feel guilty and desperate at times.

A cool breeze off the ocean blew in the open window. My solitary debate in the car had used up all my anxiety about calling. I walked over to the TV and picked up the sunglasses, then called. Rosemary answered as usual. She seemed happy to hear from me and excited about the day before. Had I read the Sunday paper? There was a long article about a woman who had been reunited with her son. It was a very positive article. She couldn't believe the coincidence. It was amazing. I told her about the sunglasses and asked if she minded my seeing Jack alone.

She completely understood. He had an hour before he had to get to work. Would it be okay if he could come now? In fact, he was already out the door and on the way!

I waited for Jack out on the little balcony. A butterfly flew up and sat poised on the railing. I heard a knock. When I saw Jack again, I felt pure delight. The words that came out of my mouth were not what I wanted to say. Instead, I launched into the story I'd rehearsed a million times, explaining why I had to give him up. All that I had read about adoptees' rights to know came babbling out of my mouth, but as I spoke, my thoughts were of the amazing sense of recognition I felt. His spirit was known to me. Though I had last seen him as an infant and he was now a grown man, I knew him, felt him. We knew each other's spirits—something other, and greater, than the mere physical entities with which the adoption laws deal.

Can any mother ever sever herself from and forget her child just because a statute directs her to do so?

When Jack finally had a chance to speak, he asked if I had considered an abortion. I was not expecting that question. But as I looked at him, I knew I had to answer honestly.

"Yes, we did. But I believe you were meant to be born. I never felt pregnant and never had a positive pregnancy test until it was

269

too late. By then, I already felt you with me. You were a strong life."

I felt awkward describing the pressure exerted by the Church and the situation in the South in the sixties that made it impossible to keep him. Kids in Los Angeles today wouldn't dream of capitulating like that. Attitudes were so different now. Perhaps Jack wouldn't believe how different?

Jack seemed to take it personally that his adoption had caused me to be estranged from the Church. He said he felt the Church was different now.

I saw I was giving him a burden he had not had before. It hurt him that I had such strong negative feelings about the Church and society. He wanted me to be happy, not sad, because of him. I didn't want him to feel burdened by my critical attitude, but I couldn't hide it either.

"Did it bother you yesterday when I called my mom Mom?" he asked. He was looking me straight in the eyes.

I winced and answered him the way I wanted to feel, but couldn't: "No, not at all. She's your mom and I am so glad that you two are so close." My eyes caught his again, after my lie. He hadn't missed a thing. I couldn't lie to him. "Yes. It did bother me. And it bothered me that it had bothered me."

"I thought so," he said.

Remembering the letter from Elinor saying he had few questions about me, I asked Jack if he had ever thought of me. He said he was beginning to recall times when he had. He especially remembered a time when he was twelve and had to bring home a terrible report card. In a moment of rebellion, knowing he would be in a great deal of trouble, he tore the report card up in pieces and threw it in the garbage on the way home. At that moment, he said, he wanted to run away and find me.

I told him that the years around twelve and thirteen were a common age at which adopted children long to find their biological mothers and fathers. They are very vulnerable years. At that age, children are beginning to figure out their own identities. Adopted kids are missing so much information about themselves that this is an almost impossible task for them.

I said that I felt he hadn't been sure whether or not he wanted to meet me. He said he hadn't known until yesterday whether he wanted to, or why. He only knew he was curious. But it had turned out to be great to be with someone so similar. He thanked me for finding him. I told him that he was teaching me a great deal about myself. There were things I saw in him that I had never acknowledged about myself before.

The hour went by quickly and he had to get to work. He asked if I wanted to have lunch with him and his mom on Wednesday. I was thrilled. The only problem was waiting until Wednesday.

I walked with Jack down to the parking garage and watched him climb into his car, hating to see him leave me. It almost felt like I had fallen in love.

Chapter Eighteen

I called Chris in Virginia and told him everything. I could only imagine what he was feeling. He had given me support through the whole search. Anytime I needed him, he was there to help. He knew more than anyone what this meant to me, because it meant the same thing to him. His loss was as deep as mine. We never spoke of this loss of our first family. We were too loyal to our families now, whom we loved. I wondered if Jack would ever have the chance to be with both of us at the same time.

The rest of the day I took long walks, recovering. I called my parents to tell them all about Jack and his family. I read the article in the L.A. *Times* Rosemary had mentioned. I shopped.

I called an old friend, Lee, who had helped me with advice as I prepared to meet Jack: "Now, just don't overwhelm him . . ." Remembering his words had kept me from going over the edge, whenever my feelings became too intense. After letting me go on and on about what an incredible child I had found, Lee laughed, "And he has ten fingers and ten toes!"

That was the feeling I was experiencing, that I thought felt the same as falling in love! I was acting just like a new mother waxing on about her miraculous infant. How funny, but it made sense. I had never had the chance to stare dreamily for hours at his infant perfection and make wishes for him as he slept in his cradle. Maybe time would help me gain control of my feelings so their intensity wouldn't threaten the people I loved.

For the rest of the week I visited friends in San Marino. Wednesday, on the way to meeting Jack and Rosemary for lunch, I found myself again battling old insecurities. Once more I felt unworthy, too unworthy to get anything I really wanted, too unworthy even to ask.

We went for lunch to a Mexican restaurant overlooking the lake where Jack worked as a lifeguard in the summers. Over and over I told myself, you just have to accept this. You may *feel* like his mother, but Rosemary *is* his mother. He doesn't know you. Yet when Jack said, "Mom, I need new Topsiders," I had to force back my instinct to jump up and run to the shoe store. My instincts were not able to tell that another mother had that role, that I must love silently, sit passively when he asked something of his parent.

To try to come to terms with reality, I took pictures. I wanted to anyway, to show everybody back home, but at first I had to force myself. When I tried to take a picture of Jack, I got so caught up looking at him, I was almost too weak to push the shutter. And it was hard to snap Rosemary and Jack in one frame, together.

After lunch, we went back to their house. Jack took pictures and broke down my defensiveness about having someone take mine. Rosemary suggested we prop up the camera and take one of the three of us together. So we did that, and then pretty soon, everything started to feel more natural. I began to enjoy myself.

We had a good day together. Jack was pretty courageous to spend an entire day with two mothers. We talked so much. We discussed all the amazing coincidences.

Jack said, "You should write a book!"

I said, "No way."

I was just getting used to telling my friends about my big secret. I couldn't imagine the world knowing. But as I looked at him, I felt so proud. He would never be a secret again.

I asked if he wanted to meet me at Brett and Kip's football camp for their last day's scrimmage on Friday. Rosemary said they would all go. She would bring her sons Mark and David, too.

I despaired of ever finding Brett and Kip, let alone Jack and his family. The huge field was packed with families, finding each other or watching the various scrimmages. There were so many people. At last I found Kip. Jack spotted us. He was carrying a cooler. Rosemary and Mark and David followed behind. Kip was quarterback and I could tell he wanted to do his best with Jack watching. Brett hadn't seen us, but he made a very impressive tackle.

After the scrimmages, we all walked back up to the dorms. Brett and Kip packed. I hoped, as I watched Rosemary's face, that my coming into their lives had added to it, not taken anything away. I hoped she knew how profoundly grateful I was to her for caring for our son.

There was an awards ceremony next, but they had to leave. We all walked out to their car and then took more pictures. I hugged Rosemary and Jack. Young David had already climbed into their car and was eyeing us warily, still worrying about our possible designs on his brother. Mark climbed in the backseat. In his own quiet way, he sighed with relief, too. Rosemary got in the passenger seat, and Jack slid in behind the wheel.

The tires crunched the gravel as the huge station wagon backed out. Jack drove slowly. Just before they disappeared, they turned and waved again and we waved back.

Kip broke the silence. "Well, there goes your son, Mom."

There was a touch of anger and a protectiveness in his voice. I looked at Kip and then Brett. I remembered the bewildered looks on David and Mark's faces. I had no way of explaining any of it to them.

I must have been daydreaming, because the ringing of the phone startled me. It was Jack. He had just returned from spending five days in Virginia Beach with Chris. I had had a feeling, when he told me he was going to New York to stay with his grandmother, that Virginia would be too close to resist.

Jack had given Chris only a half day's notice. I tried to imagine how Chris handled that shock. Jack said he himself was perfectly calm, until the plane landed. Then he felt so weak he didn't think he could get out of the seat. He said they knew each other right away. They were both very comfortable with one another and he had a great time. He liked Chris's wife, Emily, and their son Steve. The girl who had been Jack's best friend when they were nine years old (who had also gone to school with Steve) came over often. We talked for an hour and a half and it seemed like ten minutes.

No sooner had we hung up than the phone rang again. It was Chris. He was so happy, so grateful to Jack for not holding anything against him and for being so generous and loving. They had found themselves still in the kitchen well into the early hours of the morning. Emily was crazy about Jack, too, which meant so much to Chris. He said he felt he had known Jack always.

Weeks later I received a letter from Chris with pictures of Jack's visit. I was curious to see how the years had affected Chris. He hadn't changed, except his hair was gray. Chris's note said he had received a nice letter from Jack. In it Jack had expressed frustration at not being comfortable telling his parents how he felt about us after meeting us. Ironically, he now felt free to love his parents even more.

I knew he was reacting quite typically. Adopted people seemed to feel a need to protect everyone, even from their own feelings, whether or not that was necessary. Sadly, it often was necessary, however, judging from what I had heard and read.

I had sent Elinor Green pictures and kept her abreast of the progress of our reunion. She confessed it had been difficult to keep the knowledge that Jack was also in California from me. When I asked her about the disastrous first adoption placement she'd told me it was exceedingly rare for a baby to be returned. But she added that she'd often found horror stories of all sorts when she'd had to go through old records. The supply of babies was so great back then that they weren't always as careful as they should have been.

Not knowing anything about Jack's first eight months bothered me tremendously. I wanted to get Jack infant pictures of himself, to find out what his life had been like, and to give back some of the missing months to him. For a long time, I felt it was not my place to make the call. Finally, I realized that I had a right to know for my own peace of mind. I was also Jack's mother.

Grace found the name of the mother of the initial adoptive father for me. Catholic Social Services refused to send the records, so this was the only way. This time my script was well prepared.

The woman who answered the telephone was taken aback by my call, but she reacted kindly. She reassured me over and over that Jack (she kept calling him Dennis) had been greatly loved by everyone. He had been a beautiful child with the sweetest, friendliest disposition. They used to get him all dolled up in the most beautiful clothes and show him off to everyone. Unfortunately she had no pictures to send us. She apologized. I promised to send her pictures of Jack and she sent a Christmas card in reply.

———

Jack and I did not see each other again for six months, although we talked on the phone half a dozen times. He seemed to need to assimilate everything slowly. I knew I had to resist pressuring him or intruding on his family.

We were invited by friends to the Rose Bowl parade on New

Year's Day and to stay with them for a couple of days. I waited to call until I got down to Los Angeles. Rosemary said Jack was up at Tahoe and she wasn't sure when he planned on coming back.

New Year's Day my friends and the boys and I had our picture on the front page of the L.A. *Times*. But it was only of our backs, as we perched on ladders to watch the pageant. My friend, Kathy, and I decided we would stick the photo on our refrigerator doors to inspire our New Year's diets. I was about to go upstairs to finish packing, as we planned to leave in an hour for the long drive home, when the phone rang. It was Jack. He had just gotten back from Tahoe. When he heard we were leaving, he asked if we could wait. Of course we would.

We decided to go to the Santa Anita Racetrack together. I had never been before. But would Rosemary think I was corrupting Jack? Would she think I really was a wanton woman after all? I was only being paranoid, I knew. Jack said Rosemary would have no problem about his going to the racetrack.

We took it as a good omen when Virginia's Pride came in first, despite the odds. We had bet on him to win because Jack had been born in Virginia. I felt we were getting to know each other. His twentieth birthday was eight days away. At twenty, Jack was naturally striking out on his own as an independent adult. To find another mother risked doubling the task, I realized, and I tried to walk a fine line between loving support and not sabotaging his freedom.

Leaving the nest seems to be a loaded time in all families, but even more so in this kind of situation. One of the problems for families created by adoption is letting go. Some adoptive parents unconsciously fear that, because there is no biological bond, their child will never return. The adopted person, remembering unconsciously the terror of the original abandonment, fears leaving. I didn't want to make it even harder for Jack.

As I waved goodbye, I felt so much had been left unsaid. I wouldn't be seeing him again until the summer, when my mother was coming to visit. Jack had said he would come up then.

We had moved again, and the boys and I had been in our new house only a month when Mom arrived. She and I sat outside in the sunshine on the deck watching a snowy egret standing poised, motionless, in the mud of low tide, awaiting its lunch. I was sad as I resigned myself to the idea that Jack was not able to fly up to meet her. She was leaving in a couple of days; time was running out. I told her I had pretty much given up hope. As usual, she did not let any feelings show. I had tried to bring up the past to clear the air, but my attempts had been fruitless.

I got up from my chair, frustrated, and went up to my room. I quietly thought about the anxiety Jack must be feeling over coming up here. I sent him a silent message to come only if it was best for him, not to feel guilty or obligated. A half hour later, the phone rang. He was taking the three o'clock flight but could stay only one day. I asked him when he had made up his mind to come. He said only about a half hour earlier. I thanked him for doing me this big favor.

Back downstairs, out on the deck, Mom was still reading her book. I told her Jack was coming. She put down the book and mobilized herself to help me clean the house.

I met him at the airport and we drove the long way home through San Francisco to get to the Golden Gate Bridge. As we drove, Jack recalled his trips into the city to go to the theater and sightsee when they had lived in the East Bay. I could not get over the fact that he had lived so close, we could have passed each other on the street. We could have been in the theater at the same time, only a few rows apart. I could have bumped into him accidentally and not known him at all, which had always been my nightmare. Maybe I had.

When we got home, my mother and the kids were wrecks. For some reason, the Jacuzzi tub would not turn off and they were worried that the motor would burn up. Brett was upset that he was being asked by Mom to clean his room perfectly for Jack. I didn't want the kids to resent Jack for getting the royal treatment. They could not appreciate what a big deal this was for Mom. The fuss over the runaway Jacuzzi was enough to take the edge off the initial introduction.

Jack took one look at the Jacuzzi, pushed a button near the motor, and it turned off. Our relief at this dissipated some of the tension. Still, I could see that Mom was overwhelmed at seeing that Jack looked practically like my twin. This was her first grandson, and she was only now meeting him twenty years later. But she was resilient.

I had invited Cathie to join us for dinner. Since meeting at PACER, we had become good friends. I had helped her search for her mother. She had talked with her mother for the first time at my house. I would never forget Cathie's face as she made that call. She was so afraid she would be rejected. But within two minutes, they sounded like old friends. This, said Cathie, was the connection even her son Nick could not provide for her. I had had lunch with Cathie and her mother the day after they first met, and I had been mesmerized watching the two of them mirroring the most subtle gestures. Were gestures in the genes?

As she searched, all Cathie had known was that she was born to Armenians in Chicago thirty-five years before. When we had hit a real snag in the search, I suggested she go to John, the psychic, for what he could "see." John told her that her mother was in California, maybe around Bakersfield. He was off only by three hundred miles. She was in Los Angeles. Cathie felt, after meeting her mother, that had she had more information about herself and had she been able to know her mother earlier in her life, and thus understand herself better, she could have avoided many mistakes she'd made.

It was good for Jack and my mother to hear someone else's story; it made it easier to deal with our own.

On the way to the airport the next day, Jack and I were able to talk a little more deeply about the past we had shared together and what it meant for both of us to find each other again. He liked my mother and seemed quite sensitive to what Brett and Kip might be going through. Still, I had the bizarre sense that, if we could print out our empathetic communications, we would find more information than we exchanged in words. We almost didn't have to talk to understand and know.

It was different when Jack came up again to meet my father. Perhaps Dad was less nervous. After my parents' divorce, and before his remarriage, he had been involved for a while with a woman who wouldn't let him get away with not talking about things. He confessed he had been shocked that this woman felt he had done a horrible thing giving his grandson to total strangers. She told him adoption was a middle-class disease. Among the rich, the girl's mother would go away with her daughter and come back pretending the child was hers. Although no one was fooled, the game was played out and the child remained with the family. With the poor there was usually someone who could take care of the child and there was no social stigma attached to the unwed status; there were more pressing things to worry about, she'd said.

Until then, Dad said, he always believed he had done the only thing possible under the circumstances. Ironically, Dad's wife

Lucy had two adopted sons, one a year older than Jack and one a month younger. She does not think her sons have any desire to search, although she is happy for Jack and me.

I still could not tell Mom or Dad my feelings about what had happened to me and to Jack. It seemed more important that they know their own. They had done the best they knew how at the time.

Just before Jack and I had to leave for the airport, my friend Morgan came by to meet Jack and my father. She talked about what it was like for her to go to a home for unwed mothers and then give up her daughter, Beth. I watched my Dad, Lucy, and Jack listening to her tell much the same story as mine, yet it was easier for them to hear hers. They were too close to me to be able to handle it yet.

Many of us, who thought we would be able to give up our children, and had committed ourselves to do so before their birth, suffered an enormous change of heart and would have made a different decision if that opportunity had been clearly presented. But of course the authorities had known this and pressed us even harder to sign, to surrender, realizing that our overwhelming desire and need for our children threatened their arrangements. The interdiction was swift, the infants removed quickly.

Most of us could not "get on with our lives" afterwards. As many as 60 percent did not "go on and have other children." Some could not bear the pain of even looking at a baby. Lives had stopped at the moment of relinquishment. A great part of ourselves remained with our children when they were separated from us; the power of that connection was immeasurably affecting. Like the amazing coincidences involved in so many reunion stories, the wrenching emotional devastation caused by our physical separation was a kind of evidence of the undeniable spiritual strength of that bond.

This time on the way to the airport, Jack and I could finally talk directly about my giving birth to him. I told him how I used to play with him in my belly and how he used to respond, how I talked to him all the time and knew he was with me then. It was an incredibly intimate moment. And I realized that Jack had to acknowledge in words that I had given birth to him to feel comfortable with himself.

The search and reunion had become mysterious and mystical for me. I had a hunger to know more, since it seemed to me now that there was a hidden reality that I had only gotten a glimpse of. I began working with a hypnotherapist.

Rob guided me back, opening memories to me. The recollections and sensations were incredible. In one meditation, I came to a perfect point of energy that I recognized as myself.

That same spark was most visible to me in my baby pictures. This made sense; babies are closer to their true essence. I was glad to be remembering, yet still uncomfortable that there was no way to corroborate these mystical insights, until Jack's next visit happened. He brought his girlfriend, Anna, with him. This was Anna's first airplane trip. She was really excited about it. She was lively and fun. A good person for Jack.

I had told him about Rob and hypnotherapy and asked him if he was interested in the experience. I was a little uncomfortable, wondering what Rosemary would think. This was still considered pretty far out stuff by most people. Actually, I was projecting my own worries onto her. I didn't want to be responsible. I still felt my welcome was conditional. But Jack was almost twenty-one now and certainly capable of making decisions about his own life. I trusted him when he said yes.

While Jack was with Rob on Saturday afternoon, Anna and I had lunch in a Greek restaurant. She came from a huge Catholic family of nine children. Anna had a directness and a natural curiosity that helped us talk through some of the things we needed to. I felt it was as if she gave Jack the emotional ease to see me for who I really was to him and to sort out all his impressions. For her I was not a loaded issue but just me.

When Anna and I returned to the hynotherapist's office, Rob and Jack were getting along famously. Rob had asked Jack to regress to different ages in this life. When he asked him to go to six months, Jack said he was lying in a crib in a strange room. There was a woman with long brown hair sitting in a chair. She seemed to be a stranger to him and he said he felt very confused. Rob then asked him to go to his birth, and Jack said he couldn't, but immediately saw himself as a newborn baby. He said he saw me holding him and smiling down at him. He knew it was me. The room seemed all white, with tall windows and a white floor. Rob said that Jack had to have carried that memory with him at some level all of his life. I was rocked.

"I know the moment you are talking about," I said. "The nurse had brought you into the room and it was the first time you had your eyes open. And I looked into them and felt the most indescribable delight, like I was saying hello to your soul. And it seemed I had known you forever, and that I could look through your eyes and see heaven. The room had tall windows and a white linoleum floor."

.   .   .

In the fall, Jack enrolled in Fresno State. He chose that school so he could play water polo. (So that was why John had "seen" me going to Fresno.) I made the trip down there with Morgan. Her daughter Beth was also going to Fresno State. Who would have ever guessed, when we met searching for our children, that they would end up going to the same college? Beth's adoptive mother had dinner with all of us. Jack seemed relieved to be the observer this time.

Anna attended the College of Idaho on a volleyball scholarship. I was able to see Jack a couple of times as he stopped in San Francisco between connecting flights to visit Anna. And she spent the night at my home when she had to wait for her plane to leave for Idaho the next day. But Anna found she hated being so far away from Jack and her family.

Now that Jack was living on his own at school, our situation often seemed almost normal for a mother and son. But the reality became clear again at times like Christmas. He went then to another family, another home. Sharing Christmas with him would have felt natural to me. But for him we might have seemed like distant relatives. I did not know. I never wanted to ask.

Two Mother's Days had passed since we'd first talked. It still hurt when I didn't hear from Jack on that day despite my comprehension of the reality of the situation. I sent a card to Rosemary to honor our special connection. We two still talked on the phone on occasion. It was a challenge for both of us to rise above our insecurities, and trust each other.

On the third Mother's Day since I'd found Jack, he came up for the weekend because his water polo team was competing in a nearby town. On Saturday, Kip and Jack went to one of my favorite stores to buy me a Mother's Day present. The fact that they had gone together was present enough for me. The next morning, before anyone else was up I caught sight of our cat, Blackie, slinking up the stairs leading to Jack's room. Jack had an allergy to cats, so I rushed after him and caught Blackie just as he pushed open the bedroom door.

There Jack was, asleep. I had not seen him sleeping since he was two days old. This was a tremendous moment for me.

Anna decided one year at Idaho was enough and enrolled, with Jack, at Fresno. By October, they were looking for a more cosmopolitan school and came up to check out San Francisco State. Their planned one-night stay turned into four days when their little yellow VW bug broke down. I hoped they might decide to transfer to a school so close to me.

One week before Christmas I sat across the table from Jack and Anna at Gatsby's in Sausalito. Jack and I sipped beers. Anna had not wanted anything. We had just seen the movie *The Last Emperor*, the first movie Jack and I had ever gone to together. I marked firsts to replace the missing firsts. This would be the first Christmas holiday we would share since Seton House.

As we talked, I felt there was something they wanted to tell me. I wondered if they had made their decision about transfering schools yet. But we talked about other things. Anna began to question me about being pregnant with Jack. She wanted to know what it had been like for me physically, how I had lived in the home, and how I'd felt when I gave Jack up. Jack listened intently.

It was past midnight when we left Gatsby's. As tired as we were, we talked until three in the morning after we got home. But I felt we still had not talked about what was really bothering them.

The next night Morgan and Patrick had a party to which our whole family was invited. Anna and I drove to it together in my car. What was really going on that they couldn't tell me? I asked Anna what was wrong.

"Jack and I are pregnant," she said.

I nearly ran off the road. Anna said they were terrified of telling their parents. Jack felt so ashamed. They had been trying to find the courage to tell me. I was thrilled and surprised at the prospect of becoming a grandmother even though I wasn't sure I felt old enough, wise enough. I tried to reassure Anna that it would all be okay. They would have an incredible baby.

Jack was amazed that I wasn't mad at him. I was shocked that he thought I could be. Although this did not seem the ideal time for them to start a family, how could I be mad about a baby? How could I, of all people, be judgmental?

Anna waited until after her birthday in mid-February to tell her parents. Some fear in her, too, made her feel she had to wait until it was "too late to do anything about it." When Anna told her parents, they were upset initially. But then they responded from their hearts. Jack still put off telling his parents for another two weeks. Rosemary handled the news just fine, shocking Jack. And Don immediately went up to the attic to look for the baby things. Was one source of Jack's apprehension what had happened to the three of us — Jack, Chris, and me — the fear of being parted?

After finishing the semester at Fresno, Jack and Anna found a small apartment in Long Beach. Their baby was due in the middle of August. My mother was coming for a visit the last two weeks of that month. I prayed that Anna would have the baby before my mother arrived. I was afraid to share the birth with her, though I felt guilty for feeling this way.

———

On Wednesday the seventeenth, Mom and I went into the city to see the Andrew Wyeth exhibit at the de Young Museum. Before the tour was to start, we browsed through the bookstore and I bought a baby album to give Jack and Anna. The tour began at two. We rushed into the gallery so we wouldn't miss anything, but I could not attend to one word the woman was saying. My body was uncomfortable and my mind was just not there. Sometimes my eyes couldn't even focus on the pictures. The lecture lasted about an hour. Then Mom and I found the coffee shop. I was not able to pay attention to much that she was saying, and then suddenly, everything was in clearer focus than I had ever remembered. It was very strange.

We spent the rest of the afternoon at the museum and then went home to cook dinner. Just before I put the food on the table, the phone rang. Kip answered.

"A boy! Oh, wow!"

Kip talked a little with Jack and then I got on the phone.

"Congratulations, Grandma!" Jack said to me.

This had to be the greatest joy. Dylan had been born at 2:59 that afternoon. He was born with his eyes wide open, looking around at everybody. Anna was fine. We couldn't talk long; visiting hours were over and he had to leave.

We opened some champagne and sat down and the phone rang again. This time I answered. It was Rosemary.

"How does it feel to be a grandmother?"

"Great! How does it feel for you?"

"Great!"

We talked a long time as she shared every detail with me.

I had to wait until Monday to go down to L.A. with Mom to see Jack and Anna and baby Dylan. Mom's friend Gordon was coming to San Francisco for the weekend with a business colleague, and we couldn't change plans. I was wishing I could be in L.A., though.

We sat around the fire after dinner, then Mom went out on the deck for some air. Gordon's friend Lamar remarked about the pictures of my three sons. Gordon looked at me, surprised. "I didn't know you had three sons." I told him my story quickly. Lamar continued probing. "Do you ever worry sometimes that your oldest son will get someone pregnant? I always worry about my daughters."

I looked at him, helpless. Mom had never told Gordon about Jack. It was left to me to tell him that she had just become a great-grandmother.

When Mom and I drove to L.A. together on Monday, I asked her why she had never told Gordon. She said there had never been an opportunity. That's when I knew I had to give up trying to discuss the past with my mother. I would let it all go and enjoy the present with her.

She did ask me if I thought it could possibly run in the genes, getting pregnant out of wedlock. I assured her I didn't think we were a mutant strain. Plenty of people have sex before marriage. We may be an extremely fertile family, but we weren't defective.

Mother wondered what the protocol for visiting would be. Would she be accepted as Dylan's great-grandmother or would she be viewed only as a remote connection? Would Brett and

Kip be considered uncles just like Mark and David? Or would our family have to hold back the love we felt?

My sister Janice had sent Dylan the little rocker my parents had given her for her third birthday. When she realized she was going to be childless, she wanted him to have it. I knew Jack would be touched that a relative he'd never met would care.

We drove up to Jack and Anna's home in the late afternoon. Jack met us at the bottom of the steps and opened the door.

I was barely breathing as I climbed the steps. This was the greatest gift I could ever have, to see their child, my grandson.

Jack opened the door for us, and my mother went in first. Her great capacity for living in the present allowed her to be spontaneous and charming. I was mute, completely caught up in the momentousness of the occasion and rendered speechless. It was overwhelming.

He was lying in the bassinet I had given him, the one Brett and Kip had occupied. All I could see at first was a mass of dark hair. It was just like Jack's had been.

I tiptoed around to peek at his face. He looked so much like Jack had looked, like a little Indian. I was so happy. Jack would be getting a good idea of what he had looked like during the eight months that we had no record of.

Dylan began to stir and my mother picked him up. She had always been crazy about babies. All the time we were growing up, I remembered how she watched the babies in church. She got Dylan smiling right away. I finally said, "Enough, Mom. It's my turn." As I held him, Dylan's body felt so familiar to my body. Holding him somehow filled up the place that had been left empty by Jack.

At the end of the evening, after dinner was over and Dylan had been fed again, I asked Anna if she minded my holding

Dylan while he slept. We all sat peacefully together, not talking much. We were pretty tired.

I held Dylan close to my heart. I looked down at Jack, sitting on the floor. In his sleep, Dylan smiled a wise and ancient smile and I felt the circle close round us, completed.

Afterword

The first time I looked into my son's eyes, I felt like a criminal. As I unwrapped his hospital blanket and took in the fragrance of a newborn, I feared that the nurses or nuns would appear to accuse me of contaminating my own son. The three months I had spent at the home for unwed mothers had left me feeling I would be the worst person for my own child to know.

Yet the instant I looked into my son's eyes, I was stunned by their power. I felt I had known his soul for eons. At the same time, all I heard was, "If you love your baby, you will give him up. It would be selfish to keep him. In no time, you will forget, and go on to live a wonderful life and have more children."

Nineteen and a half years later, our eyes met for the second time. My son was walking down the slope of lawn in front of his parents' home. I couldn't believe the magic of that instant. As our gazes met and held I knew that our bond had endured.

My story is shared by an untold number of women who were unwed mothers, too, most of whom gave up their babies for adoption. The secrecy surrounding unwed motherhood has made it impossible to know how many millions of us there are. It is also a story shared by those who have escaped this fate. It would be difficult to find a girl who grew up during the fifties, sixties, and seventies, who wasn't anxiously aware of a nearby home for unwed mothers. Whether we lived through the experience or escaped it, we were all affected. Such homes still exist today.

My son Jack talked me into writing our story. Many times I have been tempted to give it up, overwhelmed by the emotions evoked. Each time, in the course of my work with adoptive parents, birth parents, and adoptees, I would encounter a woman who had given up her child. In her tale I would hear my story—my pain, my incomprehension at my inability to forget, my fear that I was unique in this and, therefore, crazy, my shame at what I had done in relinquishing my own child.

I know that there are so many woman who need to read about this subject to validate their own experience, to help them help themselves or to help them to seek help.

Though almost twenty-five years have passed, adoption is still being proposed by many in positions of authority as a *simple* remedy for the problem presented by an unwed mother. And the newborn has become a precious commodity to all too many. Though the relinquishing mother has more leverage today than she did in my day and can often obtain some variety of "open" adoption should she wish it, even open adoptions are no easy answer.

Unless they have had the experience of relinquishing a child, those counseling the mother cannot fully comprehend the ramifications of their advice. While adoption often may be the right answer, it cannot be lightly counseled as a simple alternative, either to abortion or to single motherhood. Mothers who give up their babies inevitably and profoundly alter the rest of their lives. Many cannot go on to lead fulfilling existences, haunted by fear for their child's welfare, guilt both for abandoning their child and for continuing to love and long for him, and shame, too, at having taken the "easy" way out. Despite desperate efforts to hide their experience some compulsively repeat it while others find themselves thereafter infertile. Some seek out punitive situations and abusive marriages to match their feelings of unworthiness. Some do become alcoholics and addicts, seeking to forget. Many become suicidal. Those who seem to succeed best in burying their feelings often find them erupting in disguise. This is a secret which cannot really be hidden. For despite all her efforts to forget, and all efforts made to forget her, the other mother continues to exist.

There is a nationwide movement to change current laws which keep adoption records sealed. Once the records are opened, it will be even more vitally important that people be prepared for the powerful issues they are dealing with so that the reunions which will ensue can be successful for everyone.

It is my hope that reading *The Other Mother* will help people to come together in love, not fear.

Appendix

The following organizations may be of help to adoptees and birth parents who wish to search for one another. They comprise a network of more than 360 search and support groups throughout North America.

AMERICAN ADOPTION CONGRESS
1000 Connecticut Avenue, NW S-9
Washington, D.C. 20036

INTERNATIONAL SOUNDEX REUNION REGISTRY
P.O. Box 2312
Carson City NV 89702

ORPHAN TRAIN HERITAGE SOCIETY
Rte 4, Box 565
Springdale AR 72764

NATIONAL ORGANIZATION FOR BIRTHFATHERS AND
ADOPTION REFORM
P.O. Box 1993
Baltimore MD 21203

PEOPLE SEARCHING NEWS
P.O. Box 22611
Fort Lauderdale FL 33335-2611
Assistance/Referral Hotline 305/370-7100

THE RESEARCHERS CLEARINGHOUSE
P.O. Box 22363
Fort Lauderdale FL 33335-2363